Analytical Grammar

Level 3
Parts of Speech
Student Worktext

Created by R. Robin Finley

ANALYTICAL GRAMMAR.

888-854-6284
analyticalgrammar.com
customerservice@demmelearning.com

Analytical Grammar: Level 3, Parts of Speech Student Worktext
© 1996 R. Robin Finley
© 2022 Demme Learning, Inc.
Published and distributed by Demme Learning

All rights reserved. No part of this book may be reproduced, stored in a retrieval system, or transmitted in any form by any means—electronic, mechanical, photocopying, recording, or otherwise—without prior written permission from Demme Learning.

analyticalgrammar.com

1-888-854-6284 or 1-717-283-1448 | demmelearning.com
Lancaster, Pennsylvania USA

ISBN 978-1-60826-646-3
Revision Code 1122

Printed in the United States of America by CJK Group
  2 3 4 5 6 7 8 9 10

For information regarding CPSIA on this printed material call: 1-888-854-6284 and provide reference # 1122-11012022

Table of Contents

Why We Learn Grammar...vii

Lessons
Lesson 1: Nouns, Adjectives, and Articles............................. 1
Lesson 2: Pronouns... 17
Lesson 3: Prepositional Phrases...................................... 31
Lesson 4: Subject & Verb... 47
Lesson 5: Adverbs.. 65
Lesson 6: Sentence Patterns 1 & 2.................................... 83
Lesson 7: Sentence Pattern 3... 99
Lesson 8: Linking Verbs and Sentence Patterns 4 & 5................. 113
Lesson 9: Helping Verbs... 129
Lesson 10: Conjunctions & Compound Situations...................... 147

Certificate of Completion 167

Reinforcing Skills... 169

Reinforcement Answer Key 205

Index 259

Bibliography 261

Level 3 | Parts of Speech

Level 3: Parts of Speech
Why We Learn Grammar

First, let's clear something up: You already know grammar. No, really! You began learning the grammar of your native language even before you could talk. Even a toddler knows that "Dad ate pizza" makes sense, while "Pizza ate Dad" is silly. So you already know grammar. You just don't KNOW you know grammar. Then why do we have to study it, anyway? Well, it's important because:

When you know the names of the different parts of speech and the jobs they do, you can make sure you are communicating clearly when you write. The most important part of writing is making sure that your intended audience, whoever that might be, can understand what you want to say.

- It helps us to understand how we can use different language and grammar in different situations if we need to. We don't talk to our teachers the same way we talk to our dog or cat, for example. But however we speak, to whomever we are speaking, grammar is neither "right" nor "wrong." It's just grammar!

The idea of "GRAMMAR RULES" may seem quite intimidating, but don't worry! We will be showing you the guidelines for one kind of grammar. Getting comfortable with how to use different grammar tools can make your writing flow a lot more easily. Sure, there are a couple of "rules," like "Every sentence must have a subject and a verb." But the only real mistake you can make is if a reader doesn't receive the message you are trying to send!

What about diagramming?

Yes, you'll learn how to diagram sentences in this program. It might look intimidating, but you will probably be surprised at how easily you learn it. It is an excellent tool for making sense of complex grammar concepts. You can actually see how different parts of speech relate to one another. Believe it or not, some people enjoy diagramming—they find it very satisfying! Once you are comfortable with the concepts, you might find that you never need to do it again, because you can do it in your head. But, if you do need to, you will be able to.

Make your own grammar book

After you work through each lesson, tear out the Lesson Notes and Application & Enrichment pages that introduce each concept and put them in a binder. Put the index from the back of your worktext in front of the pages as a guide to quickly find topics. You will have created a grammar reference book that you can use for the rest of your life. Let's get started!

Lesson 1
Nouns, Adjectives, and Articles

Lesson 1: Nouns, Adjectives, and Articles

Nouns

A noun is a word that **names a person, place, thing, or idea**.

A **common noun** is a word that names an ordinary person, place, thing, or idea. Common nouns are never capitalized and consist of one word only.

Examples:

Persons:	teacher, man, girl
Places:	school, yard, city
Things:	bridge, carrot, building, day
Ideas:	anger, democracy, inspiration*

Nouns representing ideas are often called **abstract nouns.**

> * Watch for the *-ion* ending—that's a strong indication that the word is a noun!

A proper noun is the **name** of a *specific* person, place, thing, or idea. Proper nouns are capitalized and may consist of more than one word. No matter how many words are in a proper noun, it still equals only one noun.

Examples:

Persons:	Ms. Jones, Nelson, George Washington Carver
Places:	Cranford High School; Anchorage, Alaska; Costa Rica
Things:	the Golden Gate Bridge; the NBA; Wrigley Field; April 1, 1492*
Ideas:	the Theory of Relativity, the Industrial Revolution

*All dates and years are proper nouns whether they are included in a date or by themselves. Think of them as the name for that specific day or year: not just any day, but June 30, specifically; not just any year, but 1986, in particular, for example.

Adjectives

Adjectives **modify,** or describe, **nouns and pronouns.** In English, they usually come in front of the noun they modify. Examples are *tall, silly, beautiful,* and *several.* For now, all of the adjectives you will be identifying will be next to the nouns they modify.

Watch out for **proper adjectives**! These are adjectives made out of proper nouns; for example, *England* is a proper noun, and *English* is the corresponding proper adjective. Just like the proper nouns they come from, they always begin with capital letters.

Articles

There are only three articles in English: *a, an,* and *the.* Articles always come in front of the nouns they modify, although not always directly in front of them. The article *a* is used in front of words that begin with a consonant sound (*a tree, a cat*), while *an* is used before words that begin with a vowel sound. This is decided by the word that is immediately after the article, not the noun; so, for example, *"an apple,"* but *"a big, red apple."*

Articles can be definite or indefinite. Imagine choosing an ice cream flavor from a line of tubs. You might say, "I want *the* one on the end," because that is the one you definitely want. If you are asked how you would like your ice cream served, you might say, "I would like it in *a* cone," because any old cone will do, as long as you have *the* flavor you asked for. *A* and *an* are indefinite articles because they are nonspecific. *The* is a definite article because it is specific.

When used in proper nouns or proper adjectives, articles are not capitalized unless they are the first word of the official name or title.

You've learned the names of three words: **noun**, **adjective**, and **article**. Words also do certain ***jobs***. Adjectives and articles do the job of **modifying**, or giving more meaning to, nouns, so their job is that of **modifier**. That is the only job they do. Nouns can do five different jobs! These jobs will be discussed in future lessons, so for now, you just need to identify them as nouns.

Now it's time to put your new knowledge into practice! For the first few lessons, you will be *parsing* sentences. That means identifying the parts of speech in a sentence. Here's what to do:

Step 1: Find all the **nouns** in each sentence. Write ***n*** over the common nouns and ***pn*** over the proper nouns. If a proper noun is made up of more than one word, write ***pn*** in the middle and draw lines, or "wings," over all the words in the noun (see example).

       n   *n* ————*pn*————
Example: The teenagers loved Elvis Presley's famous song, "Blue Suede Shoes."

Notice that we didn't mark *Elvis Presley's* as a noun. Head to Step 2 to find out why!

Step 2: Find all of the **modifiers** (adjectives and articles) in the sentence. Do this by going back to each **noun** you identified and asking "which?" Any word located near the noun that answers this question is either an **article** or an **adjective**. Write ***art*** over the articles and ***adj*** over the adjectives. For our example, first ask yourself "which teenagers?" *The* teenagers. We know *the* is one of the three articles, so write ***art*** above. Then do the same for the remaining nouns.

Hint: Not all nouns have modifiers.

    art *n*   ————*adj*———— *adj* *n* ————*pn*————
Example: The teenagers loved Elvis Presley's famous song, "Blue Suede Shoes."

When you ask yourself "which song?," the answer is *Elvis Presley's famous* song. The song is both *Elvis Presley's* and *famous*. Nouns can have many modifiers. What do you notice about *Elvis Presley's*? It includes a proper noun. It has been made into an adjective by adding *'s*, which shows that the song belongs to Elvis Presley. Adding *'s* is powerful—not only does it show possession, it makes a noun into an adjective! In this example, it makes a proper noun into a **proper adjective**. Mark these in the same way that you mark proper nouns, with "wings" over all of the words that are part of the proper adjective.

1 EXERCISE A

Nouns, Adjectives, and Articles: Exercise A

Directions

Step 1: Find all of the nouns. Write *n* over each common noun. Write *pn* over each proper noun. Use "wings" (—*pn*—) to include all of the words that are part of the proper noun if it's more than one word.

Step 2: Ask yourself "which?" about each noun. Write *adj* over each adjective and *art* over each article. Use wings to include all of the words that are part of a proper adjective. Look back at the lesson notes if you need help identifying any of the parts.

1) Even before the United States was a country, people played a game like baseball.

2) Baseball's rules were written down in 1845 by the Knickerbocker Baseball Club in New York City.

3) The rules of the Knickerbocker Club's game have not changed much over the years.

4) The American people couldn't get their fill of baseball!

5) Talented players like Babe Ruth, Jackie Robinson, and Lou Gehrig became household names.

Exercise A 1

Directions

Mark the nouns, adjectives, and articles like you did in the first section. Remember to use wings for proper nouns and proper adjectives that have more than one word. Look at the lesson notes if you need to.

1) Many kids wanted to play baseball like their heroes in the Major Leagues.

2) In 1939, Little League Baseball began in Williamsport, Pennsylvania, with three teams of kids.

3) Today, Little League Baseball is played by kids of all nationalities around the world.

4) The Little League World Series is held each year in countries across the globe.

5) The winning teams from each region of the world go to Williamsport for the championship tournament.

Short answer

6) Write the definition of a **noun**. Use a complete sentence.

7) Which type of noun begins with a capital letter and may consist of more than one word?

Nouns, Adjectives, and Articles: Exercise B

Directions

Step 1: Find all of the nouns. Write *n* over each common noun. Write *pn* over each proper noun. Use "wings" *(—pn—)* to include all of the words that are part of the proper noun if it's more than one word.

Step 2: Ask yourself "which?" about each noun. Write *adj* over each adjective and *art* over each article. Use wings to include all of the words that are part of a proper adjective.

1) On a cold, rainy day in December, 1891, Dr. James Naismith tried to think of a game to play with his gym class.

2) Because the class couldn't go outside, Naismith invented a new game for his students to play in the gymnasium.

3) Naismith hung a peach basket on the balcony's railing, and the students tried to throw a socccer ball into the basket.

4) The peach basket was a nuisance, because the students had to climb a ladder to retrieve the ball after each point.

5) Old soccer balls had laces that held a cover over an inflated rubber ball, causing the ball to bounce in unpredictable ways.

EXERCISE B **1**

6) As more people came to the games, some spectators in the balcony began to interfere with the ball or the basket.

7) Dr. Naismith cut the bottom from the peach basket, approved a new ball without laces, and added a backboard to protect the basket.

8) The basket's backboard changed the game by adding rebounds and layups to the players' strategies.

9) In 1958, Coach Tony Hinkle made an orange ball that spectators and players could see better than the old brown ones.

10) The game of basketball has changed a lot in the more than 130 years since Dr. Naismith's invention on a cold, rainy day in Springfield, Massachusetts.

Short answer

11) Write the definition of **adjective** in a complete sentence.

1 EXERCISE C

Nouns, Adjectives, and Articles: Exercise C

Directions

Step 1: Find all of the nouns. Write ***n*** over each common noun. Write ***pn*** over each proper noun. Use "wings" *(—pn—)* to include all of the words that are part of the proper noun if it's more than one word.

Step 2: Ask yourself "which?" about each noun. Write ***adj*** over each adjective and ***art*** over each article. Use wings to include all of the words that are part of a proper adjective.

1) In the United States, football is a different sport than the game played in the rest of the world.

2) The first American football game was played on November 6, 1869, between Rutgers and Princeton, two college teams.

3) The game played that day looked a lot like soccer, because players were not allowed to pick up the round ball.

4) The twenty-five players on each team were allowed to kick or swat the ball with their feet, hands, and head.

5) The rules that developed into American football are actually from a game that began in Canada.

EXERCISE C **1**

6) The Canadian rules called for eleven players on each side and allowed players to carry the oblong ball.

7) Pudge Heffelfinger of the Allegheny Athletic Association was the first player paid to play the new game of football, in November, 1892.

8) In 1920, the National Football League was organized by a group of professional teams called the American Professional Football Association.

9) The young NFL's rules said professional teams could not use college players or steal players from other teams.

10) A rival football league began in 1960; however, the two leagues eventually merged into today's NFL.

Short answer

11) List the three **articles** in English. Use a complete sentence.

12) Where will you find the article in a sentence, in relationship to a noun?

1 APPLICATION & ENRICHMENT

Application & Enrichment

Paraphrasing Lesson 1

In each lesson, after Exercise C, you will find an Application & Enrichment activity. These mini-lessons introduce concepts and help you practice skills to improve your writing and communication.

Some Application & Enrichment exercises will ask you to **paraphrase** something. Paraphrasing is a skill you can use all throughout your school career and for the rest of your life: in book reports, writing essays and reports, and even telling a friend about a story you read or a movie you watched! When you paraphrase, you take what someone else has created and retell it in your own words.

For this exercise, you can change as many words and phrases as you want, but try to keep the basic structure of each sentence. Look for nouns and adjectives, and then find **synonyms** (words that mean the same thing) to replace them.

Here's an example from a famous poem called "Casey at the Bat" by Ernest Thayer:

> It looked extremely rocky for the Mudville nine that day;
>
> The score stood two to four, with but one inning left to play.
>
> So, when Cooney died at second and Burrows did the same,
>
> A pallor wreathed the features of the patrons of the game.

When you're paraphrasing, you need to read and understand what the original author is trying to say. In the first line, when the author says *It looked extremely rocky...*, do they mean that the ground where the game was played had literal rocks and stones lying around? No, of course not. They're saying that the team had a difficult task ahead of them. When you need to paraphrase, read the passage several times until you are sure that you understand what the author is saying.

Here's one possible paraphrase of the stanza above:

> Things looked rough for the Mudville baseball team that day.
>
> They were down two to four in the bottom of the ninth inning.
>
> So when Cooney was tagged out at second and so was Burrows,
>
> The fans' faces became deathly pale.

Here's another example from Mark Twain's great classic *Tom Sawyer*:

> "Hello, old chap, you got to work, hey?"
>
> Tom wheeled suddenly and said:
>
> "Why it's you, Ben, I warn't noticing."
>
> "Say—I'm going in a'swimming, I am. Don't you wish you could? But of course you'd druther work—wouldn't you? Course you would!"

Tom contemplated the boy a bit, and said:

"What do you call work?"

"Why, ain't *that* work?"

Tom resumed his whitewashing, and answered carelessly: "Well, maybe it is, and maybe it ain't. All I know is, it suits Tom Sawyer."

"Oh, come now, you don't mean to let on that you like it?"

The brush continued to move.

"Like it? Well, I don't see why I oughtn't to like it. Does a boy get a chance to whitewash a fence every day?"

That put the thing in a new light. Ben stopped nibbling his apple. Tom swept his brush daintily back and forth—stepped back to note the effect—added a touch here and there—criticized the effect again—Ben watching every move and getting more and more interested, more and more absorbed. Presently he said:

"Say, Tom, let *me* whitewash a little."

One possible paraphrase:

"Hiya, buddy, got chores to do, huh?"

Tom turned around quickly and said:

"Oh! It's you, Ben! Sorry, I wasn't paying attention."

"Hey, I'm going for a swim! Bet you wish you could go, too. But I can see you're really having a great time! SURE you are!"

Tom stared at Ben for a moment.

"Why shouldn't I be having a great time?"

"Are you trying to tell me that's fun?"

Tom went back to his painting and remarked casually:

"Maybe, maybe not. All I can tell you is I enjoy it."

"Oh please, Tom, don't try to tell me you're having fun!"

The paintbrush moved slowly back and forth.

"Why not? It's not every day a guy gets to whitewash a fence!"

This was a new way to look at the situation. Ben stopped chewing his apple. Tom took a swipe with his brush—stood back to look at the results—moved forward to make a couple more dabs—moved back to look again—Ben watching like a hawk, becoming increasingly fascinated, increasingly hooked. After a few moments he said:

"Hey, Tom? Can I try it for a little bit?"

1 Application & Enrichment

Directions

Mark all of the common and proper nouns, adjectives, and articles in the following passage from the *Elmira Daily Advertiser* (Monday, July 4, 1887, p. 5). Then write a simple paraphrase of it by finding synonyms for as many nouns and adjectives as you can. You might have to look some words up in the dictionary if you don't know what they mean, and you may choose to use a thesaurus to find synonyms. Be as creative as you want, but try to keep as much of the original passage's meaning as possible.

Mark Twain's effort to umpire a game of old-fashioned baseball on Saturday afternoon at the Maple Avenue Park was not unmixed with an element of good-natured humbuggery.

Nouns, Adjectives, and Articles: Assessment

Here's your chance to show your skills by finding all of the nouns, adjectives, and articles in the following sentences. Then provide the definitions for the parts of speech you have been studying. Remember that you can look back at the notes if you are not sure.

Directions

Write **n** over the common nouns, **pn** over the proper nouns (don't forget the "wings," if necessary), **adj** over the adjectives, and **art** over the articles.

1) The game of football, or soccer, is played by more people around the world than any other sport.

2) Many people believe the game began to be called *soccer* in the United States, but the nickname originated in England in the 1880s.

3) Before that time, *football* referred to any kind of game in which a ball was kicked to score a goal.

4) Association football got its name when England's Football Association wrote down a set of rules for one type of football game.

5) To differentiate among the many games called *football*, this game was officially called *association football*.

1 Assessment

6) English college students liked to play two main games: rugby football, named after a British boarding school, and association football.

7) The students gave their two favorite games the shortened nicknames of "rugger" and "asoccer," which was shortened again to "soccer."

8) In England, "soccer" was never more than a nickname, and the game took over the name of "football."

9) In the United States, Canada, and Australia, people already played their own popular versions of different games called "football."

10) To avoid confusion, players of association football in these countries called their sport "soccer," and the name stuck.

Short answer

11) Define **noun**:

12) Define **adjective**:

13) Which kind of noun always begins with a lowercase letter and consists of only one word?

14) List the three articles in the English language:

Lesson 2
Pronouns

Lesson 2: Pronouns

A **pronoun** is a word that takes the place of one or more nouns with their modifiers. A pronoun can do anything a noun can do. Sometimes it even has its own modifiers! (These are usually adjectives; you won't often find a pronoun with an article as a modifier.) Here are a couple of definitions that will help us to talk about pronouns.

Antecedents

An **antecedent** is the noun or nouns that the pronoun stands for. Some pronouns don't have stated antecedents, because the antecedents are understood from **context**. Sometimes you will find the antecedent in a previous sentence.

Context

For our purposes, **context** is the setting or meaning of a word, sentence, or paragraph. When we are reading, we consider all words in their context, whether they are familiar or unfamiliar, by looking at their relationship to other words around them. If the words are unfamiliar, or, as with a pronoun, they are standing in for another word, we look for clues from the surrounding text to figure out what the word means. If a reader isn't able to figure out the antecedent of a pronoun from context, the sentence probably should be rewritten!

                    pn   *pro*

Example: Jasmine said she was tired.   *The word* **Jasmine** *is the* **antecedent** *for* **she.**

You don't need to memorize the following lists of pronouns, but you do need to read these lists and definitions carefully to be sure you can recognize a pronoun when you see one. You also should be aware that different kinds of pronouns are used in different situations. We'll learn more about those situations later. Right now, just focus on identifying them.

There are five main categories of pronouns in the English language.

Personal Pronouns

These pronouns occur in four "cases." Don't worry about when these cases are used yet. Just become familiar with the pronouns, enough so that you can recognize them when you see them. Personal pronouns should have clear antecedents, or they can cause confusion.

	Subjective	**Objective**	**Possessive**	**Reflexive/Intensive***
Singular	I	me	mine	myself
	you	you	yours	yourself/yourselves
	he	him	his*	himself
	she	her*	hers	herself
	it	it	its	itself
Plural	we	us	ours	ourselves
	they†	them†	theirs†	themselves†

†The pronouns on the last row—*they, them, theirs, and themselves*—are also used as gender-neutral singular pronouns when the antecedent's gender is unknown or not relevant to the context of the sentence. For example, instead of saying, "*He* or *she* should go to the bus stop after school," we should say, "*They* should go to the bus stop after school."

Indefinite Pronouns

Indefinite pronouns are those with unknown or nonspecific antecedents. We don't know what noun these pronouns are replacing. "Someone left the water running." "Does anyone really like pineapple on pizza?" "Several have yellow flowers." It's not the quantity that's indefinite (for example, "somebody" always takes the singular form of the verb—we'll get to that later!); it's the antecedent. So when we hear, "He ate three of them!" we are unsure what he ate—cheeseburgers? apples? entire pizzas?—but we know there were three. In this example, then, *three* is an indefinite pronoun.

Singular	Plural	Either
another*	both*	all*
anybody	few*	any*
anyone	many*	more*
anything	most*	none
each*	others	some*
either*	several*	
everybody	two*, three*, etc. (all cardinal numbers can be indefinite pronouns)	

The following are only **singular** and have no plural:

everyone	no one	other*
everything	nobody	somebody
much	nothing	someone
neither	one*	something

Demonstrative Pronouns

Think of pointing at something in the store display case: "What do you want?" "I want *that*." Demonstrative pronouns point something out or set it apart. These pronouns usually do not have antecedents.

Singular	Plural
that*	those*
this*	these*

Interrogative Pronouns

Have you ever heard of someone being *interrogated*? That's when someone is asked a lot of questions, usually in a formal investigation. That's where the name *interrogative pronouns* comes from—these are pronouns that are used to ask questions. They usually come in cases like the personal pronouns. These pronouns don't have antecedents and can be singular or plural.

Subjective	Objective	Possessive	No Case
who	whom	whose*	which, what
whoever	whomever	whosever*	whichever, whatever

Relative Pronouns

Relative pronouns, along with the adjective clauses they introduce, answer the questions "Who?" "What?" "Which?" about a noun. They are words you already know, and we will talk about them in Level 4 when we learn about adjective clauses. These are all the relative pronouns:

who/whom	what	which	that*

*Remember that we said that parts of speech have one name but can have many jobs? Note that several of the pronouns listed have asterisks next to them. The pronouns with the asterisks can act as adjectives at times. That's why it's best to follow the suggested order when you are parsing sentences. If you have already marked one of these words as an adjective in the sentence (if it answers the question "which?"), then it isn't acting as a pronoun in the sentence. Look at this example:

```
            pn          pro  adj    n
Example:   Jack  loaned  me  his  book.
```
Note that **his** *is being used as an adjective in this sentence: Which book?* **His** *book.*

```
            pn         art    n    pro
Example:   Jack  said  the  book  was  his.
```
Note that **his** *is being used as a pronoun in this sentence. Its* **antecedent** *is "Jack's book."*

Many words that are similar to some of the pronouns you've just studied (such as *my, your, our, their*) can **only** be used as adjectives. That's why they aren't listed with the personal pronouns. Some grammar books call these words "possessive pronouns." In this program, however, we will simply call them adjectives, since they are doing an adjective's job.

Pronouns: Exercise A

Directions

In this exercise, the focus is on personal pronouns. Personal pronouns have antecedents, although they may not be found in the same sentence. Look back a sentence or two, if needed. Pronouns are easier to identify if you find all of the nouns and their modifiers first.

Step 1: Find all of the nouns. Write *n* over each common noun and *pn* over each proper noun. (Don't forget the "wings," if necessary!)

Step 2: Ask yourself "which?" about each noun. Write **adj** over each adjective and **art** over each article. Use "wings" to include all of the words that are part of a proper adjective. Be on the lookout for pronouns that are doing the adjective job!

Step 3: Find all of the personal pronouns and write *pro* over each one. Below each sentence, write each pronoun and its antecedent.

                pn   *art* *adj*   *n*   *pro*   *pro*

Example: 1) David aimed at the distant target, but he just couldn't hit it.

      he = David   it = target

2) "I know the reason you missed the target, but do you know what it is, David?" asked Marina.

3) David looked at Marina, but he had no idea what she meant.

4) Jacob and Tom, both friends of David, were puzzled by her question themselves.

5) David muttered to himself, "Seems to me the problem must be this old slingshot."

2 EXERCISE A

6) When Marina heard his response, she chuckled to herself about it.

7) She said to David, "If you think you can hit the target, you will hit it."

8) She knew that just thinking a positive thought could have a large impact on whether he hit the target or missed it.

9) David realized she was right and wished he had thought of the idea himself!

10) David raised his loaded slingshot, thought about the bullseye, and placed a marble in the center of it.

Fill in the blank

11) A pronoun is a word which takes the place of a _____.

Pronouns: Exercise B

Directions

In this exercise, the focus is on demonstrative and interrogative pronouns, although it also includes some personal pronouns. Since demonstrative and interrogative pronouns don't usually have antecedents, you won't have to look for them.

Step 1: Find all of the nouns. Write *n* over each common noun and *pn* over each proper noun. (Don't forget the "wings," if necessary!)

Step 2: Ask yourself "which?" about each noun. Write *adj* over each adjective and *art* over each article. Use "wings" to include all of the words that are part of a proper adjective.

Step 3: Find all of the pronouns and write *pro* over each one. Remember to check the list if you're not sure if a word is a pronoun. (Be on the lookout for pronouns that are doing the adjective job! They are probably already marked as adjectives.)

1) Johnny Carson was a late-night television host, but he once made a joke that caused some trouble for him.

2) What he claimed was that there was a shortage of paper towels in this country.

3) He went on to describe what the consequences of this shortage might be, which alarmed many people who listened to him.

4) The implication of this joke was that people had better stock up on paper towels quickly or face the consequences.

5) This was a humorous skit to those who knew a shortage of paper towels did not exist.

2 EXERCISE B

6) Within days, however, a real shortage developed, which was surprising!

7) Those who did not realize there was not a real shortage went out and bought up all of the paper towels they could find.

8) This disrupted the normal distribution, which created shortages for whoever really needed paper towels.

9) Whoever believed the shortage to be true acted on it and, by their actions, caused the belief to become true.

10) This is another example of a self-fulfilling prophecy which came about because of what people thought.

Fill in the blank

11) A pronoun is a word which _____ of a noun.

12) A noun is the name of _____.

13) An adjective _____.

14) An antecedent is _____.

Pronouns: Exercise C

Directions

This exercise is designed to give you practice with the indefinite pronouns, but all of the other pronouns are included, too. Remember to refer to your notes if you need help.

Step 1: Find all of the nouns. Write **n** over each common noun. Write **pn** over each proper noun. Use wings to include all of the words that are part of a proper noun, if necessary.

Step 2: Ask yourself "which?" about each noun. Write **adj** over each adjective and **art** over each article. Use wings to include all of the words that are part of a proper adjective.

Step 3: Find all of the pronouns and write **pro** over each of them. Be careful—there is one pronoun that needs wings!

1) Many who are successful at what they do in life have a positive mental attitude.

2) Everyone knows that students in our school have positive and creative attitudes.

3) All of us believe our school is the best, and, because we think it is the best, we act

   in ways that make it the best.

4) Everyone who visits our school is impressed by the friendly, helpful students and faculty.

5) All of us work to keep our halls and cafeteria clean so everyone can enjoy them

   as much as we do.

2 EXERCISE C

6) When we see someone who is careless about our school, we remain positive and do whatever we can to correct the problem.

7) Hundreds of people watch our sports teams, but no one has ever accused us of poor sportsmanship.

8) Anyone who has a question or problem can always get help from a teacher, a counselor, or a principal.

9) We cannot manage everything at one time, so we manage one thing at a time.

10) Often, if someone believes they can do something, they will do it!

Fill in the blank

11) A pronoun _____.

12) The three articles are _____.

Application & Enrichment

Paraphrasing Activity 2

We learned a little about paraphrasing in the Application & Enrichment activity in Lesson 1. It is an essential skill to be able to process information and put it into your own words, because using other writers' words is called **plagiarism**. Plagiarism is taking someone else's words or ideas and presenting them as your own. This can include just changing words while keeping the structure of the sentence. That's why it is so important to read and read and read a passage until you understand it and can put it into your own words. Look at the following example from Mark Twain's *A Connecticut Yankee in King Arthur's Court*:

> "It was in Warwick Castle that I came across the curious stranger whom I am going to talk about. He attracted me by three things: his candid simplicity, his marvelous familiarity with ancient armor, and the restfulness of his company—for he did all the talking. We fell together, as modest people will, in the tail of the herd that was being shown through, and he at once began to say things which interested me."

Here is a "paraphrase" that is actually plagiarism:

> It was in Warwick Castle that I met the odd fellow whom I am going to tell you about. He fascinated me by three characteristics: his honest directness, his amazing acquaintance with old armor, and the peacefulness of his presence—for he did all the speaking. We ended up together, as humble folk will, at the end of the line that was being taken on the tour, and he immediately started to speak of things that intrigued me.

The sentences are all the same; they just have a few different words! Now look at this paraphrase of the same passage:

> I met the unusual man that I want to tell you about while I was visiting Warwick Castle. Both of us, not being the pushy type, were hanging to the back of the tour group when he began to give interesting commentary on what we were seeing. I was fascinated with his wealth of knowledge about ancient armor, and his straightforwardness and pleasantness made me like him right away, even though I couldn't get a word in.

It is clearly the same passage, but the sentence structure, word choice, and even the sequence that the information is presented in is different from the original.

Directions

In Lesson 1's Application & Enrichment, you replaced the adjectives and nouns in the following sentence to make it different. Mark all of the nouns (***n***), adjectives (***adj***), and articles (***art***) again, and mark any pronouns (***pro***), too. Next, reread the sentence until you are sure you know what it says. Finally, cover the sentence and rewrite it in your own words. You can change words, sentence structure, or anything else you would like, as long as you try to provide the same information in your rewritten sentence as is given in the original.

Mark Twain's effort to umpire a game of old-fashioned baseball on Saturday afternoon at

the Maple Avenue Park was not unmixed with an element of good-natured humbuggery.

2 Assessment

Pronouns: Assessment

Directions

Mark all of the nouns (***n***), proper nouns (***pn***), adjectives (***adj***), articles (***art***), and pronouns (***pro***). Be sure to use wings, if necessary. Remember that you can look at the notes pages if you need help.

1) Sofia once said to me, "Aya, if you think something is true, even if it isn't, you can make it become true."

2) Many people have accomplished impossible things simply because they thought they could do them.

3) Humans love stories of everyday people who do impossible things because they believe in themselves.

4) This is a popular theme of folktales and fables: the brave hero or lucky fool who accomplishes an impossible task.

5) Because they did not believe that the task was impossible, they thought creatively and found a way to do it.

6) Folktales are full of characters who are given impossible tasks to complete and who refuse to believe they can't do them.

7) King Arthur didn't know that he shouldn't have been able to pull the sword from the stone, so he tried and he succeeded.

8) Greek mythology has many stories of human heroes who were given impossible tasks by those who hoped they would fail.

9) Japanese folklore tells of two sisters who found a way to wrap fire and wind in paper so they could earn their freedom.

10) Every country in the world has stories of brave heroes and lucky fools who succeed at impossible tasks because they are positive they can do it!

2 Assessment

Fill in the blank

11) A noun is the name of _____.

12) A proper noun always begins with _____.

12) A _____ noun can only consist of one word, but a _____ noun can be more than one word.

13) The articles are _____.

14) An adjective modifies _____ and _____.

15) A pronoun _____.

15) A pronoun _____.

16) An antecedent is _____.

Lesson 3
Prepositional Phrases

Lesson 3: Prepositional Phrases

A preposition is a word used to show the relationship between two nouns.

Example: The package under the tree is mine. (under is the preposition)

The package in the tree is mine. (in is the preposition)

The package near the tree is mine. (near is the preposition)

Notice how the relationship between the package and the tree changes when the preposition is changed. Changing the preposition moves the package!

How to find a preposition

Think: anywhere a mouse can go! Most prepositions will fit into the following little sentence:

"The mouse goes _____ the box (or boxes)."

This handy little sentence will identify the majority of prepositions. Try it with the ones used in the example sentences above. They fit, don't they? If you can use a word in this sentence that describes where the mouse is in relation to the box, you know it could be a preposition.

But remember that we said "most"? There are some prepositions that don't fit. There are nine very common ones that we use all the time in our language, which may seem like a lot to remember. Here's a little memory aid: you may not be able to remember all nine, BUT AL DOES!

B = but (but me) **A** = as (as a fox) **D** = during (during recess)

U = until (until lunch) **L** = like (like a dog) **O** = of (of your homework)

T = than (than the others) **E** = except (except that one)

S = since (since breakfast)

Phrases
A phrase is a group of words that work together as a unit to express a concept.

A preposition is **not** a preposition unless it's in a prepositional phrase. A word may fit into the mouse-box sentence and look like a preposition, but the job it's doing in the sentence means that it's not acting as a preposition at the time. In that case, the word is almost always an **adverb** (which we will learn about in Lesson 5). Don't worry, there aren't any trick questions about "preposition or adverb?" in this lesson!

Practice

Use the mouse-box sentence or "BUT AL DOES" to test each word. Mark the prepositions with an *X*.

_____ between   _____ what

_____ but   _____ above

_____ about   _____ when

_____ then   _____ beyond

_____ and   _____ without

To find a prepositional phrase, you say the preposition and ask, "what?" You are looking for a noun or pronoun that answers that question. That noun or pronoun is called the **object of the preposition**.

                     art   n   pp art   n

Example: The dog barked (at the cat).   *Note: When you're parsing, put parentheses around the whole prepositional phrase.*

We know that *at* is a preposition, because it fits into the mouse-box sentence (a little awkwardly, but it fits). So we ask the question, "*at* what?" The answer is "*cat*" (strip out all the modifiers so you have just the noun; *the* isn't part of the answer). *Cat* is the object of the preposition.

Each prepositional phrase will:

- begin with a preposition
- end with a noun or pronoun
- contain only prepositions, nouns, and modifiers

If there are any other words between the preposition and its object, they are modifiers (articles or adjectives) of the object. **No other kinds of words can be in a prepositional phrase.**

In the first example of this lesson, the prepositional phrases are *under the tree*, *in the tree*, and *near the tree*. **Tree** is the object of the preposition in all three phrases.

Because a phrase is a unit, prepositional phrases have a job to do as a unit: **they are always modifiers.** If a phrase is not acting as a modifier, it can't be a prepositional phrase.

Look at these sentences:

I ate my lunch **before recess**.	(The prepositional phrase is **before recess**; *before* is a preposition and *recess* is the object of the preposition.)
I ate my lunch **before**.	(*Before* isn't acting as a preposition in this sentence because there's no object. If you ask, "before what?", there's no answer.)
I ate my lunch **before I saw you.**	(Again, *before* isn't acting as a preposition. If you ask, "before what?", the answer would be "before I saw you." That's not a prepositional phrase, because there are other words besides nouns/pronouns and modifiers. A verb will never be in a prepositional phrase.)

3 Student Notes

Practice
Put parentheses around the prepositional phrases in these sentences. Remember that a prepositional phrase must have a preposition and a noun or pronoun (plus any modifiers of the noun/pronoun). It must also answer the question "(**preposition**) what?"

1) The movie was exciting, like the reviews said.

2) The movie was exciting, like the book.

3) I like exciting movies.

4) Our exam was less difficult than the last one.

5) Our exam was less difficult than we thought it would be.

6) I cannot marry you, for I love another.

7) I cannot marry you for two reasons.

Now, parse the prepositional phrases you have identified, marking prepositions (**pp**), nouns (**n**), pronouns (**pro**), and modifiers—articles (**art**) and adjectives (**adj**). All of the words in a prepositional phrase must be one of these parts of speech. Are there any words within the parentheses that can't be marked as one of these parts of speech? If there are, it is not a prepositional phrase, and the word that looks like a preposition is not doing a preposition's job in the sentence.

Diagramming

Sentence diagramming is a tool we use, much like drawing pictures. We use diagrams to make it easier to see concepts that might be difficult to understand. Diagrams consist of three types of lines:

Horizontal	Vertical	Diagonal
—	│	\

The basic diagram of a prepositional phrase looks like this:

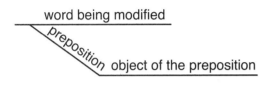

Example: the class (after my lunch hour)
            art n   pp   adj adj   n

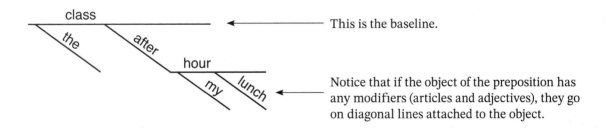

← This is the baseline.

Notice that if the object of the preposition has any modifiers (articles and adjectives), they go on diagonal lines attached to the object.

> A few prepositions consist of more than one word. They are *because of, on account of, in spite of, regardless of, according to, instead of, contrary to,* and *out of.* If you find one of these prepositions, label it **pp** and use wings to include all of the words (like you do with proper nouns).

Prepositional Phrases: Exercise A

Directions

Step 1: Find all of the nouns. Write *n* over each common noun. Write *pn* over each proper noun. Use wings to include all of the words that are part of a proper noun, if necessary.

Step 2: Ask yourself, "which?" about each noun. Write *adj* over each adjective and *art* over each article. Use wings to include all of the words that are part of a proper adjective.

Step 3: Find all of the pronouns and write *pro* over each of them.

Step 4: Find all of the prepositions and write *pp* over them. Put parentheses around all prepositional phrases, being sure to include the preposition (*pp*), the object (*n*, *pn*, or *pro*), and any modifiers of the object.

Once you have parsed the sentence, use a separate sheet of paper to diagram the prepositional phrases in each sentence. The first sentence has been done for you as an example. Don't worry about what word the phrase is modifying yet; just draw a blank baseline.

Some of the words in the sentences have been underlined. After you finish parsing and diagramming, you will be asked a question about these words.

                      pp adj   n   pro   art adj   n   pp   n

Example: 1) (In math class,) we use a certain method (of thinking).

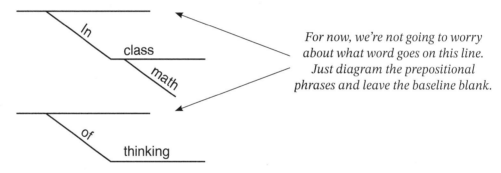

For now, we're not going to worry about what word goes on this line. Just diagram the prepositional phrases and leave the baseline blank.

2) People think a person with a <u>mind</u> for <u>math</u> has an advantage over other <u>people</u>.

3) Such people appear to learn concepts about mathematical <u>principles</u> easily.

4) They solve problems in <u>math</u> quickly.

5) Emotional blocks in your <u>mind</u> can prevent success in <u>math</u>.

6) A belief in your ability as a mathematician gives you a better chance at success.

7) The "gift" of mathematical ability exists in all people.

8) A lack of success with certain problems seldom indicates a lack of ability.

9) In school, we look for the key to success in mathematics.

10) Instead of "special" brains with ability in math, we need more confidence in our own ability!

Short answer

11) All the underlined words in this exercise are doing the same job. Look at your notes and write what that job is.

   _____

Prepositional Phrases: Exercise B

Directions

Step 1: Find all of the nouns. Write *n* over each common noun. Write *pn* over each proper noun. Use wings to include all of the words that are part of a proper noun, if necessary.

Step 2: Ask yourself "which?" about each noun. Write *adj* over each adjective and *art* over each article. Use wings to include all of the words that are part of a proper adjective.

Step 3: Find all of the pronouns and write *pro* over each of them.

Step 4: Find all of the prepositions and write *pp* over them. Put parentheses around each prepositional phrase.

Once you have parsed the sentence, use a separate sheet of paper to diagram the prepositional phrases in each sentence.

Some of the words in the sentences have been underlined. After you finish parsing and diagramming, you will be asked a question about each of these words.

1) Would you be surprised to learn that calculators were used before the discovery of electricity?

2) There is an ancient calculating tool called an abacus that has been used for thousands of years!

3) In countries in the Near East, abacuses have been used for business for many centuries.

4) Abacuses are still used today in many cultures.

5) Skilled users of an abacus can calculate at speeds similar to those of calculator users.

6) What we picture as an abacus is made of movable beads on rods in a rectangular frame.

7) There are <u>many</u> different types of abacuses.

8) Some have strings instead of wires and knots instead of beads.

9) Others have trays with sections for small <u>stones</u> that are moved from place to place.

10) The <u>Chinese</u> word for abacus means "counting tray," and that is a good name for it!

Directions

The underlined words in these sentences are doing one of two jobs. Choose your answer from the jobs below and write what job each underlined word is doing.

modifier *object of the preposition*

Sentence #	Word	Job
1	electricity	
2	calculating	
4	cultures	
5	abacus	
7	many	
9	stones	
10	Chinese	

3 EXERCISE C

Prepositional Phrases: Exercise C

Directions

Parse the sentences by marking all of the nouns (***n***), proper nouns (***pn***), adjectives (***adj***), articles (***art***), pronouns (***pro***), and prepositions (***pp***). Put parentheses around each prepositional phrase.

Once you have parsed the sentence, use a separate sheet of paper to diagram the prepositional phrases.

Some of the words in the sentences have been underlined. After you finish parsing and diagramming, you will be asked a question about these words.

1) Contrary to popular belief, you use your imagination in math class.

2) Early in the history of mathematics, the imagination of mathematicians led to the discovery of each new mathematical theorem.

3) The act of mathematical creation involves the use of all one's abilities.

4) In most cases, the gift of logic plays only a part in the mathematical process.

5) In your classes at school, success in mathematics requires an intuitive sense of the rightness of things.

6) You often give the solution to the problem an "educated" guess.

7) Sometimes you find the answer without conscious awareness of the creative process.

8) In your mind, you instinctively know the answer to the problem.

9) Creativity exists in all aspects of math.

10) The <u>logical</u> part of your mind is not the only intellectual tool in use.

Directions

Write what job the underlined words are doing in the sentence. Choose your answer from the following jobs:

modifier   *object of the preposition*

Sentence #	Word	Job
2	mathematicians	
3	one's	
5	intuitive	
5	rightness	
10	logical	

Application & Enrichment

Reading for Context

How many words do you think there are in the English language? Would you be surprised to learn that it's over 170,000?* There are an additional almost 50,000 *archaic* words that we don't use anymore. And each native English speaker only uses about 20,000–30,000 words on a regular basis. The more you read, the more words you will come across that you don't know! In a lot of cases, carefully reading the sentence and passage that the unfamiliar word is in can give you **context** clues to the word's meaning; you can get a pretty good idea of the meaning without having to look it up.

For example, we used the word *archaic* in the third sentence above: "There are an additional almost 50,000 *archaic* words that we don't use anymore." Read the sentence again, carefully. What do you think *archaic* means?

_____ Now, look up the definition or ask your instructor.

Note: If an exact meaning is important, don't guess! Get out your dictionary or look up the meaning online!

The following sentences each contain an archaic English word in a modern English sentence. Reading for context, write your guess for what the word means. Then look up the meaning of the word and write the definition in the second blank. See how close you can get to the real meaning, but don't look it up until you've guessed!

1) I shouldn't have eaten the food from the street vendor because now I am *liverish*.
   liverish
   your guess: _____ meaning: _____

2) The dog *groked* at me unblinkingly the entire time I was eating my hamburger, silently begging with his eyes.
   groked
   your guess: _____ meaning: _____

3) The old woman's *grimalkin* daintily licked its paws, cleaned its face, and curled up in front of the fireplace for an afternoon nap.
   grimalkin
   your guess: _____ meaning: _____

4) Since it was too dark to see, I *grubbled* under the car seat for my phone as best I could.
   grubbled
   your guess: _____ meaning: _____

5) Honestly, I wasn't happy with anything hanging in my closet; I can't be expected to show up on the first day of school with only these *habiliments* to choose from!
   habiliments
   your guess: _____ meaning: _____

6) Because we did not want to be followed, we *jargogled* the directions so they were useless.
   jargogled
   your guess: _____ meaning: _____

7) Juan works very hard during the week, but on Saturdays, he is *otiose* to the point of not getting dressed, not showering, and not washing dishes all day.
   otiose
   your guess: _____ meaning: _____

8) The big truck sped through the slushy puddle, *besmirching* my brand new white jacket with a splash of muddy snow.
   besmirch
   your guess: _____ meaning: _____

9) After listening to the children *brabble* for an hour about whose turn it was to sit by the window, Mom threatened to turn the car around.
   brabble
   your guess: _____ meaning: _____

10) The oxen pulling the *wain* could barely move it, because it was so loaded down with heavy sacks of grain.
    wain
    your guess: _____ meaning: _____

*2nd Ed Oxford English Dictionary 2020

3 ASSESSMENT

Prepositional Phrases: Assessment

Directions

Mark all of the nouns (***n***), proper nouns (***pn***), adjectives (***adj***), articles (***art***), pronouns (***pro***), and prepositions (***pp***). Be sure to use wings, if necessary. On a separate sheet of paper, diagram the prepositional phrases. Remember that you can look at the notes pages if you need help.

1) Men have no advantage over women in mathematical ability.

2) The perception of math as a masculine domain stems from other myths about the subject.

3) Ability in math is seen as the triumph of cool, impersonal logic.

4) This fits with an outdated, stereotypical image of men.

5) In some cases, students will not readily admit to difficulty with math.

6) Others, early in their schooling, begin believing in personal inadequacy as a reason for failure.

7) All of these students, regardless of gender, may be expressing the same fears about math.

8) Throughout history, a variety of people have contributed to the <u>field</u> of mathematics.

9) Women's historical contributions in this area are being recognized at last in award-winning films and in popular <u>nonfiction</u> books.

10) <u>Educated</u> people no longer believe that math comes more easily for men than for women.

Fill in the blank

11) The noun or pronoun at the end of the prepositional phrase is called the _____.

12) Pronouns are words that _____.

13) A proper noun begins with a _____.

14) A common noun ☐ can ☐ cannot consist of more than one word.

3 Assessment

Directions

Write what job the underlined words are doing in the sentences. Choose your answer between the following:

modifier *object of the preposition*

Sentence #	Word	Job
1	ability	
2	subject	
3	cool	
4	men	
5	some	
6	inadequacy	
7	these	
8	field	
9	nonfiction	
10	Educated	

Lesson 4
Subject & Verb

Lesson 4: Subject & Verb

In English, there are two kinds of main verbs: action verbs and linking verbs. This lesson covers action verbs. We'll talk about linking verbs in Lesson 8.

First, here are some important definitions:

Action verb

Like its name suggests, an action verb expresses physical or mental action.

Example 1: (physical action)   jump, carry, search, run, examine

(mental action)   worry, think, believe, consider

Subject

A verb has a subject. The subject is the noun or pronoun that is doing the action of the verb. To find the subject of a verb, you ask, "Who or what (say the verb)?"

          art   n   pp art   n   av   pp   art adj   n
Example 2:   The horse (in the lead) raced (across the finish line).

The verb, or action, is **raced**. Who or what **raced**? The **horse raced**. So **horse** is the subject of **raced**.

> **Tip:** Neither the subject nor the verb will ever be inside a prepositional phrase!

Some sentences will have words that look like a verb but don't have a subject. These are called **verbals**. We'll learn all about verbals in Level 4, but for now, just mark them with a **v**. If it does have a subject, then it's a real verb, and for now, mark it **av**.

          pn   av —v— art pn pp adj   n
Example 3:   Joe hopes to get an A (on this test).

"To get" looks like a verb, but if you ask, "Who or what *to get*?", there is no answer in the sentence. A subject and verb always work together. "Joe hopes" sounds right because the noun and verb work together. That's because "Joe" is a third person singular noun and "hopes" is a third person singular verb. But "Joe to get" just doesn't work together, does it?

> **Tip:** Many verbals end in *-ing*, and any verb with *to* in front of it (like *to get* in our example above) is always a verbal—more about verbals in later lessons.

Here are a few more useful definitions:

Sentence

A sentence expresses a complete thought. It must *always* have a subject and a verb, or it's not a sentence. A sentence can be either a statement or a question (exclamations and commands are just different types of statements).

          art   adj   adj   n   av   pp art   n
Example 4:   The sleek, black dog barked (at the moon).

Simple subject

The simple subject is the noun or pronoun that is doing the action of the verb, without any modifiers. In Example 4 above, **dog** is the simple subject of the sentence.

Predicate

In a sentence, a predicate is everything that is not the subject. So in our example about the sleek, black dog, the predicate is **barked at the moon**.

Simple predicate

The simple predicate is just the verb by itself, without any modifiers. In the example above, **barked** is the simple predicate. (We'll learn about verb modifiers in the next lesson.)

Diagramming

You have already started doing a little diagramming with the prepositional phrases in the previous lesson. Now we're going to learn how to diagram complete sentences! For the rest of the lessons that include diagramming, we will call going through the steps and diagramming the sentence "The Process." Don't worry, we will start slowly, and you're already familiar with the steps to take to get started. We will be adding a new step to help you identify the verb. Each of the answers to the questions asked in the steps has its own place in a sentence diagram.

I) How to Diagram the Subject and Verb

A diagram shows the structure of a sentence by making a picture of it. Every diagram starts with a **baseline** which holds the subject and verb. A baseline looks like this:

This is what it looks like when you add a short sentence to it:

Example I:

Notice that the baseline is a horizontal line and that the subject and verb are separated by a short vertical line that crosses the horizontal line.

> In a sentence diagram, capitalize the first word of the sentence, but don't include punctuation.

II) How to Find the Subject and Verb

First, parse the sentence by following all of the steps you have been using to find nouns (**n**), articles (**art**), adjectives (**adj**), pronouns (**pro**) and prepositions (**pp**), putting parentheses around prepositional phrases.

Second, mark any word that looks like a verb with a **v**. For each **v**, ask, "Who or what (say the verb)?" The answer, a noun or pronoun, will be the subject of that verb. For this lesson, when you find the subject, mark its verb with **av** for **<u>action verb</u>**. (Remember that some words that look like verbs will be verbals and will not have subjects. Just leave those words marked with **v**.)

Now that you have identified the subject and verb, write the simple subject and simple predicate (remember, that's the verb) on the baseline.

Example II: Before diagramming anything, parse the sentence.

           adj   n   av   adj   n   adj   n
           My uncle runs five miles every morning.

- The verb is **runs**.

- Ask, "Who or what runs?" Answer: **uncle**. Because **runs** has a subject, you can mark it with **av**. (If there were more verbs without subjects, you would just leave them marked **v**.)

- The simple subject is **uncle**. The simple predicate is **runs**. Write these on your baseline.

III) How to Diagram Articles and Adjectives

Articles and adjectives are diagrammed on diagonal lines attached under the noun or pronoun they modify. They should be diagrammed in the order in which they appear in the sentence.

           adj   adj   n   av

Example III: Our special guest sang.

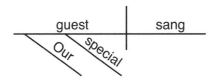

IV) How to Diagram a Prepositional Phrase

If a prepositional phrase modifies a noun, it will answer the question "which?" just like the other modifiers (articles and adjectives) you've learned. In this lesson, if a prepositional phrase modifies the subject, you will diagram it. In the first example sentence we used in this lesson, ***The horse in the lead raced across the finish line***, the prepositional phrase ***in the lead*** tells you which horse. Here's how you will diagram that:

Example IV: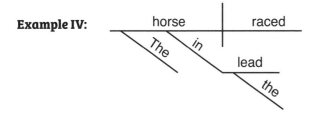

For now, don't worry about diagramming prepositional phrases that are modifying words other than the subject.

V) How to Diagram a Command

Diagramming a command or request might appear tricky because it seems there is no subject.

                        av   adj   n

Example V: Brush your teeth.

The verb is **brush**, but if you ask "Who or what brush?" the sentence doesn't say! For commands or requests, the subject is an understood "you." That means that, without saying it, it's clear that the sentence is talking about "you." The diagram will look like this:

Notice that **you** is in parentheses. That shows that it is "understood." That means that we know to whom the command is addressed. Also notice that **Brush** is capitalized; that shows that it is the first word in the sentence.

VI) How to Diagram an "Inverted" Sentence

Inverted sentences are sentences that begin with **here** or **there**.

                      av   art   n

Example VI: Here comes the principal.

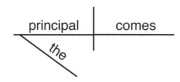

We use these sentences all the time in English, but they could be confusing to diagram. Once you find the verb **comes** and ask "Who or what *comes*?", it's clear that the subject is **principal**. It can seem confusing, because you're used to seeing the subject in front of the verb. That's why we call these sentences "inverted," which means "turned upside down."

The chart on the next page, which we call "The Process," shows the mental steps you must go through to analyze a sentence's grammar. We will be adding steps to this chart, but for now, it only includes the ones you already know.

The Process

Step 1. Find and mark **n** over all the nouns in the sentence (**pn** over proper nouns, with wings, if needed).

Step 2. Find all the articles (**art**) and adjectives (**adj**)—ask, "Which (noun)?" Remember to use wings over all of the words of a proper adjective, if needed.

Step 3. Find all the pronouns (**pro**).

Step 4. Find all the prepositions (**pp**) and put parentheses ( ) around the prepositional phrases.

Step 5. Find all words that look like verbs and mark them **v**.

Step 6. For each **v**, ask "Who or what (verb)?"

No answer? It's a verbal. Leave it marked **v** and move on.

Answer? It's an action verb.* Mark it with **av**. The answer to your question is the simple subject. The action verb is the simple predicate. Draw a baseline and fill in the simple subject and the simple predicate.

Complete your diagram with the modifiers that go with the simple subject (don't forget prepositional phrases).

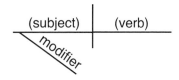

*The next few lessons focus on action verbs only, so you can mark all verbs you find that have subjects as **av**. In Lesson 8, you will learn about another kind of verb.

Subject and Verb: Exercise A

Directions

Steps 1–4. Parse the sentences by marking all of the nouns (*n*), proper nouns (*pn*), adjectives (*adj*), articles (*art*), pronouns (*pro*), and prepositions (*pp*). Put parentheses around each prepositional phrase.

Step 5. Find all words that look like verbs and mark them with *v*.

Step 6. Ask, "Who or what (verb)?" If there is an answer, mark the verb as an action verb (*av*) and fill in the baseline of your diagram with the simple subject (the answer to the question) and simple predicate (the action verb).

Diagram the subject, its modifiers, and the action verb, using a separate sheet of paper, if necessary. You don't need to diagram anything else at this point.

1) People from Mexico settled in Texas starting in the seventeenth century.

2) These people came to Texas before the settlement by the Europeans.

3) They established farms and ranches in the territory.

4) These early settlers plowed the land.

5) Their crops grew in the harsh Texan climate.

6) These Texans gave Spanish names to their towns.

7) They called one of these towns San Antonio.

4 Exercise A

8) Mexican culture spread from Texas throughout the <u>southwestern</u> United States.

9) There went these early Texas pioneers.

(See Lesson Notes, Section VI)

10) The names of these states <u>resulted</u> from the influence of these Spanish-speaking settlers.

(See Lesson Notes, Section IV)

Fill in the blank

11) A verb cannot be an action verb unless it has a _____.

12) The articles in English are _____, _____, and _____.

Directions

Write what job the underlined words are doing in each sentence. Choose your answers from the following:

subject   object of the preposition   verb   modifier

Sentence #	Word	Job
1	People	
1	Mexico	
4	These	
6	towns	
8	southwestern	
10	resulted	

Subject and Verb: Exercise B

Directions

Complete Steps 1–4 of The Process. Next, identify all of the words that look like verbs and mark them with **v**. Then ask, "Who or what (verb)?" until you find the subject and action verb. Mark the action verb with **av**. The action verb is the simple predicate. Finally, diagram the simple subject and its modifiers and the simple predicate. You don't need to diagram anything else yet.

1) Roberto Felix Salazar wrote a poem about the early Mexican settlers of Texas.

2) These people settled the land known as Texas.

3) This Mexican-American poet wanted to tell the story of the contributions of these Texas pioneers.

4) This joyful, passionate poem describes these hard-working farmers and ranchers.

5) They built their thick-walled adobe houses from the dry Texas earth.

6) Devout Catholic people struggled mightily to build their churches.

7) Strong Mexican pioneers sacrificed to make homes for their families.

8) Read this poem at your first opportunity.

   (See Lesson Notes, Section V)

9) These brave Mexican settlers left a rich legacy.

4 EXERCISE B

10) The soft Spanish names of their <u>towns</u> survive to this day.

Fill in the blank

11) If there are any words between a preposition and its object, they are _____.

12) _____ can consist of more than one word.

13) If a word looks like a verb but doesn't have a subject, it's a _____.

Directions

Write what job the underlined word is doing in each sentence. Choose your answers from the following:

subject   *object of the preposition*   *verb*   *modifier*

Sentence #	Word	Job
1	Roberto Felix Salazar	
3	poet	
4	describes	
5	adobe	
6	struggled	
7	families	
8	Read	
10	towns	

Subject & Verb: Exercise C

Directions

Complete Steps 1–4 of The Process. Next, identify all of the words that look like verbs and mark them with *v*. Then ask, "Who or what (verb)?" until you find the subject and action verb. Mark the action verb with *av*. The action verb is the simple predicate. Finally, diagram the simple subject and its modifiers and the simple predicate. You don't need to try to diagram anything else yet.

1) Today we study the contributions to American culture from all sorts of people.

2) Roberto Felix Salazar took obvious pride in his ancestors.

3) "The Other Pioneers" by Roberto Felix Salazar celebrates the accomplishments of these Texas pioneers.

4) Mexican-Americans in the southwestern United States identify with these rugged people.

5) Settlers from all nations left their mark on the Texas landscape.

6) American students try to learn about all of the different contributions to our culture.

7) Here on the land remain the marks of these early settlers.

(See Lesson Notes, Section VI)

8) Mexican-American culture really shapes the life of the American Southwest.

4 Exercise C

9) Poems like this one help us to understand more about our country.

10) Please read these stories and poems about our <u>ancestors</u>.

Fill in the blank

11) In a diagram, a _____ goes on a diagonal line attached to another word.

12) Pronouns are words that _____.

13) Adjectives are words that _____.

Directions

Write what job the underlined word is doing in the sentence. Choose your answers from among the following:

subject   *object of the preposition*   *verb*   *modifier*

Sentence #	Word	Job
1	sorts	
2	took	
3	these	
4	people	
5	Texas	
8	shapes	
10	ancestors	

Application & Enrichment

Comma Splices

The reason we study grammar and punctuation is to learn how to communicate our ideas in ways that our readers can easily understand. Punctuation provides guidance to those readers so that they know when a thought is complete, what information is essential to the idea, and even what your attitude is about what you are writing.

Level 5 of *Analytical Grammar* focuses on many different punctuation and word usage rules, but now that you can define a sentence, you can be aware of a very common, confusing punctuation error that can detract from understanding. It's called a **comma splice**.

Commas are the "yield" signs of punctuation. When used correctly, they tell your reader to mentally pause in the flow of the text. When used incorrectly, however, they can cause your reader to stumble and interfere with clear communication.

To splice is to join two things together so that they become one thing. For example, two ropes can be spliced together by weaving the strands of one rope with the strands of the other so that the two parts become one rope.

A **comma splice** is when you use only a comma to join two sentences. Comma splices are sometimes called **run-on sentences**, and it's easy to see why. Look at this example:

> We spent the whole day at the beach, we had the sunburn to prove it!

We spent the whole day at the beach and *we had the sunburn to prove it* are both independent clauses. They are complete sentences on their own, so we have two sentences that run together ("run on") with no clear stopping and starting point. When you write a sentence with a comma splice, your reader is faced with jumbled-together ideas that have a pause rather than a full stop between the end of one thought and the beginning of the next.

There are several ways we could fix this problem.

- Just write two separate sentences:
  We spent the whole day at the beach. We had the sunburn to prove it!

- Join the sentences with a conjunction, such as *and,* after the comma:
  We spent the whole day at the beach, and we had the sunburn to prove it!

- Join the sentences with a subordinating conjunction, such as *since* (Level 4):
  Since we spent the whole day at the beach, we had the sunburn to prove it!

- Join the two sentences with a semicolon (Level 5):
  We spent the whole day at the beach; we had the sunburn to prove it!

While you won't learn about numbers 3 and 4 until later lessons, you can start using numbers 1 and 2 right now!

4 APPLICATION & ENRICHMENT

Directions

The following sentences include a comma splice. Fix the comma splice by rewriting each sentence in two ways: First, write it as two sentences, using a capital letter at the beginning and a period at the end of each sentence. Next, include a conjunction after the comma. Choose from **and, but,** or **or** for this exercise, since we haven't studied conjunctions yet.

1) The bees are busy with the flowers in the garden, they are happily buzzing around.

2) I hope the baseball game is played today, it's raining really hard right now.

3) My cat got out of the house yesterday, she was as frightened as I was!

4) We might go to the pool today, we might go to the movies if it rains.

5) I will loan you my favorite book, I want to make sure you read it.

Subject & Verb: Assessment

Directions

Mark all the nouns, proper nouns, articles, adjectives, pronouns, prepositions, action verbs, and verbals in the following sentences. Put parentheses around the prepositional phrases. Then, on a separate sheet of paper, diagram the simple subject and simple predicate of each sentence. Add the modifiers for the subject to your diagram, including any articles, adjectives, and prepositional phrases.

Remember to use your notes if you need help.

1) Study this beautiful poem about Texas's early settlers.

2) Students of American culture read the literature of all our poets.

3) They want information about America's early settlers.

4) Students in this school read examples of this type of literature.

5) They want more information about their roots.

6) An understanding of our roots helps us to understand ourselves.

7) Many inquisitive Americans appreciate the numerous contributions of America's different cultural groups.

4 Assessment

8) The best writers in America created a great body of work on this subject.

9) Great literature about our early ancestors gives us pride in ourselves.

10) Here comes that positive self-esteem from our ancestors!

Fill in the blank

11) A verb is a "real" verb when it has a _____.

12) The articles in English are _____, _____, and _____.

13) Which kind of noun begins with a capital letter? _____

14) Which kind of noun consists of only one word? _____

15) A pronoun is a word that _____.

16) Adjectives are words that _____.

17) If a word looks like a verb but doesn't have a subject, it's a _____.

Assessment 4

Directions

Write what job the underlined words are doing in the sentences. Choose your answers from among the following:

subject   *object of the preposition*   *verb*   *modifier*

Sentence #	Word	Job
1	Study	
2	American	
3	settlers	
4	Students	
5	more	
6	understanding	
7	groups	
8	work	
9	gives	
10	self-esteem	

Lesson 5
Adverbs

Lesson 5: Adverbs

An **adverb** is a versatile **modifier** that can modify a **verb**, an **adjective**, or another **adverb**.

Let's discuss the parts of speech an adverb can modify.

1) When an adverb modifies a **verb**, it tells you in **one word** "how?", "when?", "where?", or "why?" about that verb.

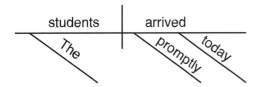

Example 1:   The students arrived promptly today.

What does *promptly* tell you? It tells you **how** the students *arrived*. It is an adverb, so it is marked **adv**.

What does *today* tell you? It tells you **when** the students *arrived*. It is also an adverb and is also marked **adv**.

Here's how we diagram adverbs. It should look familiar, except that rather than modifying a noun like our other modifiers do, these modifiers are modifying a verb.

Adverbs that modify verbs can be moved!

This is extremely important and that's why we're going to make such a big deal about it! This fact will be extremely helpful to you when it comes to figuring out what an adverb modifies. Words in English usually have to be in a certain place in a sentence (for example, articles must come before nouns, subjects usually come before verbs, and prepositions usually come at the beginning of a prepositional phrase) but that's not true of **adverbs that modify verbs**. You can almost always move such adverbs to two or three different places in the sentence without it sounding odd or changing the meaning in any way. Let's try it with the sentence in Example 1, above. Can *promptly* be moved around? How about *today*?

   a) Today the students arrived promptly.

   b) The students promptly arrived today.

   c) The students arrived today promptly.

All of these variations make complete sense, don't they? There are probably a few more that we aren't listing here, too. So if you find a word in a sentence that can be moved without changing the sentence's meaning, that tells you two things about that word:

   a) It's an adverb, and

   b) It modifies the verb!

If there's an adverb that **can't** be moved away from another word without changing the meaning of the sentence, that means that it is modifying that word and needs to stay where it is. That brings us to the other two parts of speech that an adverb can modify.

2) Adverbs that modify **adjectives** tell you "how?" or "to what extent?" about the adjective.

                      art   *adv*   *adj*   *n*   *av* *pp* *art*   *adj*   *n*

Example 2: The extremely nervous patient sat (in the dentist's chair).

What does *extremely* tell you? It tells you **how** nervous. *Nervous* is an adjective describing the patient, and *extremely* is an adverb modifying *nervous* by telling you HOW nervous the patient was. Try moving *extremely* to other places in the sentence. It changes the meaning, doesn't it? In fact, it doesn't even make sense anywhere else in the sentence. That's how we know that it is an adverb modifying an adjective, not a verb. Placed anywhere else in the sentence, it changes the meaning, and it doesn't even make sense!

Here's how you will diagram an adverb modifying an adjective.

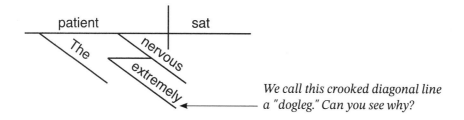

We call this crooked diagonal line a "dogleg." Can you see why?

Remember those prepositions that aren't prepositions that we mentioned in Lesson 3?

Now you're ready to know more about them, because you know what an adverb is!

                    art   *n*   *av*   *pp?*   *pp*   *art*   *n*

Example: The man drove away (from the house).

Away sure looks like a preposition, doesn't it? It often is. But it's not in a prepositional phrase in this sentence (it doesn't have an object), so it can't be a preposition. It's an **adverb**, because it's telling us *where the man drove.* There is a prepositional phrase: ***from the house.*** It also answers the question, "Where did the man drive?" In this case, we do have a preposition (*from*), because it has an object of the preposition (*house*).

So remember: if you see a stray word that looks like a preposition but doesn't have an object, it's probably an adverb!

3) Adverbs that modify other adverbs tell you "how?" or "to what extent?" about that adverb.

                    adj   n   av   adv   adv

Example 3:   Our guest left quite abruptly.

First, what does ***abruptly*** tell you? It tells you how your guest **left**. *Abruptly* is an adverb that modifies the verb *left*. Our guest didn't take their time saying their goodbyes—they *left abruptly*. What does *quite* tell you in this sentence? It tells you **how abruptly** our guest left. It wasn't just abruptly, it was **quite** abruptly! *Quite* is an adverb because it is modifying another adverb, *abruptly*. Try to move it away from the word *abruptly*. It doesn't make sense anywhere else in the sentence. That is your way to double-check.

Diagramming an adverb that is modifying an adverb also uses a dogleg, this time attached to the adverb it is modifying.

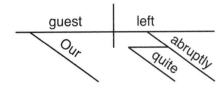

> Use a dogleg every time you have a modifier that modifies another modifier.

In fact ...

Prepositional phrases can modify verbs and other modifiers, too! You can use the same questions to test them: "how?", "when?", etc. If they answer the question, they are acting like an adverb, and you will use a dogleg to diagram them. Here's how that looks:

                    pro av   n   pp art   n

Example 4A: We ate lunch (in the park).

                (*in the park* tells you where we *ate*)

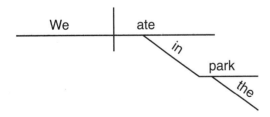

We know that *in the park* must modify the verb *ate* because we can move it to other places in the sentence and the meaning doesn't change. *In the park we ate lunch* still tells us the same thing.

                     pro av   pro   adv pp art   n

Example 4B: I saw him later (in the day).

(*in the day* tells you "later when?" or "later to what extent?")

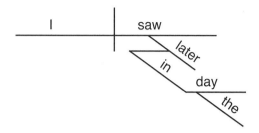

In the day can't be moved away from its position following *later* without changing the meaning of the sentence or making it nonsense. So we know that, since it can't be moved away, this prepositional phrase is modifying *later*.

> **A few more notes**
> - Many adverbs end in *-ly*. In English, you can change many adjectives (for example, *beautiful*) into adverbs by adding the suffix *-ly* (*beautifully*). Not all adverbs end in *-ly*, however, and not all words that end in *-ly* are adverbs. Only adjectives with the added *-ly* suffix are adverbs.
> - The words *how, when, where,* and *why* are often adverbs, so mark them that way for now while parsing and diagramming sentences.
> - If you really can't figure out what a word is, there's a good chance that it's an adverb!

Here's one more check you can do to determine what's being modified:

When you're having a hard time figuring out where a modifier (adverb or prepositional phrase) goes, try saying the modifier together with the word you think it modifies. For instance, in Example 4b, *saw in the day* doesn't sound right, but *later in the day* does! This tells you that *in the day* goes with *later*. Add this to the movability trick and using the questions (*how, when, where,* or *why*), and these three methods will almost always show you what an adverb or a prepositional phrase is modifying.

Adverbs: Exercise A

Directions

Mark all of the nouns (**n**), proper nouns (**pn**), adjectives (**adj**), articles (**art**), pronouns (**pro**), and prepositions (**pp**) in the paragraph below. Put parentheses around the prepositional phrases. Identify all of the words that look like verbs and mark them with **v**. Then ask, "Who or what (verb)?" until you find the subject and action verb. Mark the action verb with **av**. The action verb is the simple predicate. Mark all adverbs with **adv**. Use your notes if you need help. The first one is done for you.

                 pro   av   —————pn————— pp art adv adj   adj   pn

Example: We recognize Dr. Martin Luther King, Jr. (as a truly great Black American).

1) Dr. King certainly had a brilliant, well-disciplined mind.

2) At a very young age, King sadly experienced prejudice.

3) The White children always played separately from the Black children.

4) This bothered young Martin deeply.

5) He always wondered about the unequal treatment of his people.

6) At fifteen, King proudly enrolled at Morehouse College in Atlanta.

7) Dr. King worked diligently for his future in life.

8) He finally chose the ministry as his profession.

9) Young Dr. King always inspired his congregation with his fiery sermons against injustice.

Fill in the blank

10) A pronoun is a word that _____ .

11) An antecedent is _____ .

12) Adverbs are words that modify _____ , _____ , and _____ .

13) If an adverb can be moved within a sentence, it modifies a _____ .

14) If an adverb cannot be moved, it modifies _____ .

Directions

Write what job the underlined word is doing in the sentence. Choose your answers from the following:

subject *object of the preposition* *verb* *modifier*

Sentence #	Word	Job
Example	American	*object of the preposition*
1	certainly	
2	age	
3	always	
4	This	
5	treatment	
6	enrolled	
8	finally	
9	fiery	

Adverbs: Exercise B

Directions

Complete Steps 1–6 of The Process. Then mark all adverbs with **adv.**

Be on the lookout—there is a sneaky preposition made up of two words in today's sentences! Look back at the notes for Lesson 3 if you need help finding it.

On a separate sheet of paper, diagram the simple subject, simple predicate, and all of their modifiers (adjectives, adverbs, and prepositional phrases). You don't need to diagram anything else at this point.

1) Martin Luther King, Jr. ultimately graduated from Morehouse College.

2) He then received a scholarship to Crozer Theological Seminary.

3) The teachings of Mahatma Gandhi totally fascinated Dr. King.

4) With nonviolent methods, Gandhi successfully freed his people from British domination.

5) King sincerely believed in the success of this method.

6) He studied hard for his doctoral degree at Boston University.

7) Upon his graduation, Dr. King started his adult life as the very young pastor of a church in Alabama.

8) At that time in our history, the law mandated the separation of the races.

9) In his Sunday sermons, Dr. King <u>bravely</u> denounced these unjust laws.

10) Because of Dr. King's words, the <u>Black</u> leaders in the community also favored the use of Gandhi's methods.

Short answer

11) Which kind of noun begins with a lowercase letter and consists of only one word?

12) If a word looks like a verb but it doesn't have a subject, what is it called?

13) If you find a verb and ask, "Who or what (say the verb)?", what are you looking for?

Directions

Write which job the underlined words are doing in each sentence. Choose your answers from the following:

subject *object of the preposition* *verb* *modifier*

Sentence #	Word	Job
1	Martin Luther King, Jr.	
2	received	
3	totally	
4	methods	
5	success	
6	He	
7	pastor	
8	history	
9	bravely	
10	Black	

Adverbs: Exercise C

Directions

Complete Steps 1–6 of The Process. Then mark all adverbs with **adv**.
On a separate sheet of paper, diagram the simple subject, simple predicate, and all of their modifiers (adjectives, adverbs, and prepositional phrases). You don't need to diagram anything else at this point.

1) Dr. King's <u>message</u> about non-violent resistance to segregation laws certainly struck a chord in the hearts of many Americans.

2) <u>Mrs. Rosa Parks,</u> with a simple act of bravery, provided an opportunity for the implementation of Dr. King's plan of action.

3) Against the laws of her city, Mrs. Parks simply sat in a "Whites Only" <u>section</u> of a city bus.

4) The city police <u>quickly</u> arrested her for her "crime."

5) Dr. King promptly <u>organized</u> the Black citizens of that city in a bus boycott.

6) The Selma Bus Company soon <u>suffered</u> the daily loss of money.

7) Now Dr. King <u>led</u> non-violent marches in protest against these completely unjust laws.

8) Finally, on November 12, 1956, the United States Supreme Court issued a decision in support of these civil rights crusaders.

9) In Washington, D.C., in 1963, Dr. King delivered a very beautiful and now historic speech about his dream of racial equality for America.

10) Tragically, in 1968, a White ex-convict ended the life of this truly great American hero.

Fill in the blank

11) The three articles are _____.

12) A proper noun begins with a _____ and may consist of _____.

13) An action verb expresses _____ and must have a _____.

14) If a word looks like a verb but doesn't have a subject, it's a _____.

5 EXERCISE C

Directions

What jobs are the underlined words doing in the sentences? Choose your answers from among the following:

subject *object of the preposition* *verb* *modifier*

Sentence #	Word	Job
1	message	
2	Mrs. Rosa Parks	
3	section	
4	quickly	
5	organized	
6	suffered	
7	led	
8	November 12, 1956	
9	now	
10	ex-convict	

Application & Enrichment

Synonyms Activity 1

As we've already discussed, there are over 170,000 words in the modern English language, but we only use about 20,000-30,000. Many common words have **synonyms**, or other words that mean (almost!) the same thing. We say *almost* because there are often very subtle differences between the synonyms, particularly with verbs, adjectives, and adverbs. Having the ability to replace a general word with a specific synonym that says exactly what you mean adds spice and interest to your writing. For example, read the following sentences:

Mom is *mad* at us for playing the same song fifty times in a row.

We get it: Mom is not pleased with us. Now look at the following sentences with synonyms in place of *mad*. Rank them in order of how *mad* Mom is, with 1 being "eh, she's not that mad," up to 5 being "oops, we went too far—beware the wrath of Mom!"

_____ Mom is *annoyed* with us for playing the same song fifty times in a row.

_____ Mom is *furious* with us for playing the same song fifty times in a row.

_____ Mom is *irritated* with us for playing the same song fifty times in a row.

_____ Mom is *livid* with us for playing the same song fifty times in a row.

_____ Mom is *exasperated* with us for playing the same song fifty times in a row.

You can probably make an argument for a slightly different order than the one we provided in the solutions, but nonetheless, a *furious* Mom is more angry than an *annoyed* Mom. The sentences subtly change in meaning based on our word choice. That's why it's a good idea to practice the skill of finding synonyms for commonly used words in our writing.

5 APPLICATION & ENRICHMENT

Directions

Using a thesaurus, dictionary, or online resource, find three good quality synonyms for the following words. What we mean by "good quality" is words that you could actually use in your writing. For fun, find one outlandish synonym, too: one you would probably never use, but that's just a fun—or funny!—word!

	quality synonym 1	quality synonym 2	quality synonym 3	just for fun!
big	*immense*	*gigantic*	*substantial*	*commodious*
said				
good				
sad				
happy				
very				
nice				
many				
interesting				
walked				

Bonus word: This is a word we tend to use a lot today to describe things that are really good or exciting. Can you come up with three quality synonyms (not *good* or *exciting*) and one just for fun?

awesome				

Adverbs: Assessment

Directions

Complete Steps 1–6 of The Process. Then mark all adverbs with ***adv***.

On a separate sheet of paper, diagram the simple subject, simple predicate, and all of their modifiers (adjectives, adverbs, and prepositional phrases). You don't need to diagram anything else at this point.

Remember to look at your notes if you need any help; also remember that adverbs modifying the verb can be anywhere in the sentence!

1) The crowds at the Lincoln Memorial joyfully received Martin Luther King, Jr.

2) All Americans take tremendous pride in this beautifully eloquent speech.

3) Many Americans in that generation instantly hailed him as a hero.

4) Today, his courage inspires Americans of all colors.

5) Dr. King emphasized discipline as a very important aspect of the struggles against injustice.

6) Dr. King reminded Americans of the guarantee of equality for all people in our Constitution.

7) Constitutionally, the Founding Fathers formed this country as a home for all people.

5 ASSESSMENT

8) <u>People</u> from all corners of the world come to this sweet land of liberty.

9) Tragically, James Earl Ray <u>robbed</u> America of the life of this truly great man.

10) Today, Americans of all <u>colors</u> remember the courage of this man of peace.

Fill in the blank

11) A noun is the name of _____.

12) A _____ noun begins with a lowercase letter.

13) A _____ noun begins with a capital letter.

14) A _____ noun can consist of only one word.

15) An adjective is a word that _____.

16) The articles in English are _____, _____, and _____.

17) A pronoun is a word that _____.

18) An antecedent is _____.

19) A word may look like a preposition, but it's not unless it has a(n) _____.

20) Adverbs modify _____, _____, and _____.

Directions

Write what job the underlined words are doing in the sentences. Choose your answers from among the following:

subject   *object of the preposition*   *verb*   *modifier*

Sentence #	Word	Job
1	crowds	
2	speech	
3	hailed	
4	Today	
5	aspect	
6	Dr. King	
7	home	
8	People	
9	robbed	
10	colors	

Lesson 6
Sentence Patterns 1 & 2

Lesson 6: Sentence Patterns 1 & 2

Now that you know the basics of diagramming, the next step is to learn about the **five basic sentence patterns.** No matter how different sentences may look, no matter how complicated or how simple they seem, they all fall into one of five patterns. We have already learned about **action verbs**. The first three sentence patterns contain **action verbs only**.

To make it easier to identify sentence patterns, first remove all of the modifiers: articles, adjectives, adverbs, and prepositional phrases. Strip the sentence down to just nouns and verbs.

Pattern 1: N-V

A diagram of the N-V pattern only has two items on the baseline: a subject (**N**) and an action verb (**V**). The presence of these two parts of speech is the minimum requirement for a sentence: it must have a subject and a verb. You have already been diagramming some of these sentences, beginning in Lesson 4! The simple subject and simple predicate may have modifiers, and there may be prepositional phrases, but **there will be no other nouns or verbs**.

                 art   n   av   pp   art   adj   n

Example 1:   The boy stood (on the boat's deck).

As you have already learned, this sentence should be diagrammed like this:

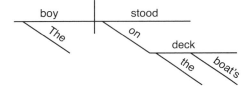

Pattern 2: N-V-N

For this pattern, we need to introduce a new job that nouns can do. It's called a **direct object**. If the subject is a noun that is ***doing*** the verb's action, the direct object is the noun that has the verb's action ***done to it***. The direct object is receiving the action of the verb. If a sentence is Pattern 2, after you remove all the modifiers you will be left with two nouns and a verb. All of these parts of speech may have their own modifiers, but there will be no other nouns or verbs in the sentence.

To figure out which noun is the direct object:

- First find the subject and verb.
- Say "(subject)(verb) what?"

The answer will be a noun or pronoun that is called the **direct object**.

                 adj adj   n   av art adj   n

Example 2:   My best friend had a birthday party.

When we remove all the modifiers, we are left with *friend*, *had*, and *party*. Start with the verb to find the subject. **Who or what** had? ***Friend*** had. So *friend* is the subject. *Friend* had **what**? *Friend* had ***party***. *Party* is the direct object.

The diagram for this Pattern 2 sentence looks like this:

Notice that the vertical line between subject and predicate extends below the baseline, while the vertical line between the verb and the direct object does not.

The Process

Now we can add another step to The Process that we introduced in Lesson 4. Step 7 is asking "(subject) (verb) what?" to determine if there is a direct object. Here's the updated flowchart for this lesson.

Step 1. Find and mark *n* all the nouns in the sentence (*pn* for proper nouns).

Step 2. Find and mark all articles (*art*) and adjectives (*adj*) by asking, "which (noun)?"

Step 3. Find and mark all the pronouns (*pro*).

Step 4. Find and mark all the prepositions (*pp*). Put parentheses around all prepositional phrases.

Step 5. Find and mark any word that looks like a verb (*v*).

Step 6. Ask, "Who or what (verb)?"

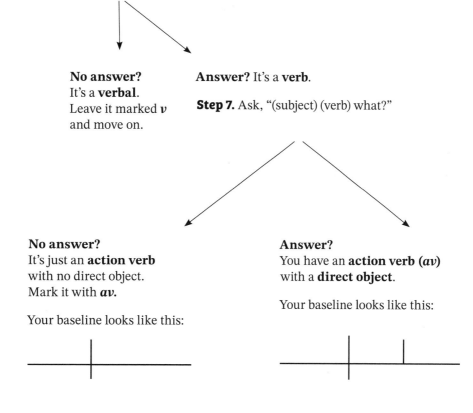

6 EXERCISE A

Sentence Pattern 1: Exercise A

Directions
All of the sentences in this exercise are Pattern 1. Parse them and put parentheses around the prepositional phrases. Then diagram the subject, verb, and all of their modifiers. You know how to diagram every part of speech in these sentences—be proud of all that you have learned so far! Remember that you can use your notes if you need help.

1) Many Americans' grandparents live in other states.

2) Many of us go to our grandparents' houses very rarely.

3) People in former generations seldom moved to other places with the frequency of today's families.

4) Most American children lived in the same town as their grandparents.

5) They visited often in their grandparents' homes.

6) During these long, frequent visits they learned about the lives of their grandparents.

7) Children in America today visit with their grandparents during short vacations.

8) Families from all economic levels move frequently from place to place.

9) A lucky few visit with their grandparents for a long time.

10) Before the <u>end</u> of your grandparents' lives, speak to them of your gratitude for all their love.

(See Lesson 4 Notes, Section V.)

Fill in the blank

11) Pronouns are words that _____.

12) To find the direct object, you say the _____, say the _____, and ask _____.

13) A word that looks like a verb but doesn't have a subject is a _____.

6 EXERCISE A

Directions

Write what job the underlined words are doing in the sentences. Choose your answers from among the following:

subject　　　*object of the preposition*　　　*verb*　　　*modifier*

Sentence #	Word	Job
1	grandparents	
2	go	
3	places	
4	lived	
5	their	
6	grandparents	
7	visit	
8	levels	
9	few	
10	end	

Sentence Pattern 2: Exercise B

Directions

All of the sentences below are Pattern 2, so all of them have direct objects. Parse the sentences and put parentheses around the prepositional phrases.

Now diagram the entire sentence. Remember to use The Process Chart in the notes and follow the steps to find the subject, verb, and direct object. Strip down the sentence by removing all of the modifiers (articles, adjectives, adverbs, and prepositional phrases). Use the proper baseline shown in Step 7. We've given you some help on the first one.

1) In today's youth-oriented society we seldom appreciate the wisdom of our elders.

   What is the verb? _____

   Ask, "Who or what (verb)?" _____
   The answer to this question is the subject.

   Ask, "(subject) (verb) what?" "_____ what?" _____
   The answer to this question is the direct object.

2) The past gives many valuable lessons for our modern lives.

3) Young people today rarely show their appreciation for the lessons of the past.

4) Older people sometimes lack patience with younger people.

5) These conflicts occasionally cause misunderstandings between generations.

6) An enjoyable hour with an older person opens doors from the past for you.

6 Exercise B

7) These doors from the past shed <u>light</u> on things in our often confusing world.

8) Some older people in <u>nursing</u> homes never get visits from younger people.

9) A visit like this benefits <u>both</u> of you!

10) <u>Take</u> time out of your busy life for a visit with an older person.

(See Lesson 4 Notes, Section V.)

Exercise B 6

Directions

Write what job the underlined words are doing in each sentence. Choose your answers from the following:

subject *object of the preposition* *verb*
modifier *direct object*

Sentence #	Word	Job
1	wisdom	
2	past	
3	appreciation	
4	Older	
5	misunderstanding	
6	person	
7	light	
8	nursing	
9	both	
10	Take	

6 EXERCISE C

Sentence Patterns 1 & 2: Exercise C

Directions:

The sentences below are either Pattern 1 or Pattern 2. Parse the sentences and put parentheses around the prepositional phrases.

Use The Process Chart in the notes and follow the steps to find the subject, verb, and whether there is a direct object. Strip down the sentence by removing all of the modifiers (articles, adjectives, adverbs, and prepositional phrases). Then choose the correct baseline for either Pattern 1 or Pattern 2. Diagram the entire sentence.

1) Rudolfo A. Anaya wrote a story about his grandfather.

2) This old farmer lived in a valley on the Pecos River in New Mexico.

3) Anaya's culture teaches respect for elders.

4) He lived on his grandfather's farm during the summer.

5) His uncles also lived in that valley beside the grandfather's farm.

6) Anaya's grandfather used few words for advice.

7) "Pray for rain."

8) Beside his grandfather in the wagon, young Rudolfo drove into town for supplies.

9) The beloved <u>grandfather</u> of his childhood died after a long, useful life.

10) Anaya gained a great <u>deal</u> of wisdom from his close association with his grandfather.

Directions

Write what job the underlined words are doing in each sentence. Choose your answers from among the following:

subject *object of the preposition* *verb*
modifier *direct object*

Sentence #	Word	Job
1	story	
2	farmer	
3	elders	
4	grandfather's	
5	also	
6	advice	
7	Pray	
8	drove	
9	grandfather	
10	deal	

Application & Enrichment

Synonyms Activity 2

Synonyms add spice and interest to our writing. Using specific, descriptive words instead of general words helps to create a mental picture for the reader that shows exactly what we are describing. Here is a sentence with some pretty generic words:

> The vehicle drove on the roadway.

Come up with three more specific words for each of the following words. We've given you an example to help you get thinking. Be creative!

vehicle	bicycle		
drove	wobbled		
roadway	trail		

Now, plug your specific words into the sentence:

along

Example: The <u>bicycle</u> <u>wobbled</u> ~~on~~ the <u>trail</u>.

Notice that we changed the preposition *on* to *along* because *along the trail* communicates what we want to say better than *on the trail*, in our opinion. Don't just plug in your words without looking at how they work in the entire sentence! If you want to change an existing word, just cross it out and write your new word above.

1) The _____ _____ on the _____.
      (vehicle)   (drove)   (roadway)

2) The _____ _____ on the _____.
      (vehicle)   (drove)   (roadway)

3) The _____ _____ on the _____.
      (vehicle)   (drove)   (roadway)

Look at your new sentences and compare them to the original. Do they paint a more vivid mental picture for a reader? Ask your instructor for their opinion.

Keep these words handy, because we will use them for the Application & Enrichment activity in Lesson 7!

Sentence Patterns 1 & 2: Assessment

Directions
Parse the sentences below and put parentheses around the prepositional phrases. Then, on a separate sheet of paper, diagram the entire sentence. Remember to use The Process. You can look at your notes if you need help.

1) An old man sat quietly on a <u>bench</u> in the park.

2) <u>Some</u> boys from the neighborhood played a game of baseball in a nearby vacant lot.

3) Paul hit the <u>ball</u> over the fence onto the old man's bench.

4) "The baseball from our game <u>fell</u> onto your bench."

5) "Your baseball nearly hit <u>me</u> on the head!"

6) In a polite tone, Paul <u>apologized</u> to the old man.

7) "You certainly have <u>very</u> nice manners."

8) "I played baseball as a <u>boy</u>."

9) The kind old <u>man</u> on the bench returned the baseball.

6 ASSESSMENT

10) A real friendship between the two grew from this chance <u>encounter</u> in the park.

Directions

Write what job the underlined words are doing in each sentence. Choose your answers from among the following:

| subject | object of the preposition | verb |
| modifier | direct object | |

Sentence #	Word	Job
1	bench	
2	Some	
3	ball	
4	fell	
5	me	
6	apologized	
7	very	
8	boy	
9	man	
10	encounter	

Lesson 7
Sentence Pattern 3

Lesson 7: Sentence Pattern 3

Sentence Pattern 3: N-V-N-N

This pattern introduces a new job that nouns can do: the **indirect object**. An indirect object is the noun or pronoun *for* whom or *to* whom an action is performed.

Start by parsing the sentence, then strip it down, removing all of the modifiers. Sentence Pattern 3 consists of four main parts in this order: the **subject (N)**, an **action verb (V)**, an **indirect object (N)**, and a **direct object (N)**. All four of these parts may have modifiers, and there may be prepositional phrases in the sentence, but once these are removed, there are **no other nouns or verbs**.

After you strip down the sentence, count the number of nouns or pronouns left over. If you have one noun left over, you have a Pattern 1 (N-V) sentence. If you have two left over, it's a Pattern 2 (N-V-N) sentence. If you have three nouns left over, you have Pattern 3 (N-V-N-N): the first noun is the subject, the second is the indirect object, and the third is the direct object.

> A sentence can't have an **indirect object** unless it has a **direct object**!

Look at this sentence to see what this looks like in action:

```
                    pn    av   pro  art   n    pp    n
```
Example 1:   Mom gave me   a dollar (for candy).

If you strip down this sentence, what is left?

Mom   gave   me   dollar

What is the verb? ***gave***

Who is doing the action of the verb? ***Mom***

What did she give? ***dollar***

Whom did she give it TO? ***me***

Below is how you diagram a Pattern 3 sentence:

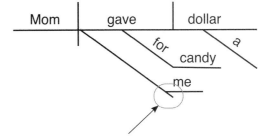

Notice the little "tail."

It looks very similar to the way we diagram prepositional phrases, but notice that it has a little tail. Do you remember that we called the way we diagram prepositional phrases a "dogleg"? Well, we call the way we diagram an indirect object a "broken dogleg" because of the little tail!

> **Important Note!**
>
> The **indirect object** will ALWAYS be located **between** the verb and the direct object in the sentence. The words will **always** come in this order:
>
> *subject – verb – indirect object – direct object*
>
> Pattern 3 sentences will only contain **action verbs**.
>
> If you have three nouns left after you strip the sentence down, the middle one is always the indirect object.

Sentence Pattern 3: Exercise A

Directions

All of these sentences are Pattern 3 sentences. Parse them and put prepositional phrases in parentheses. Strip each sentence of all of the modifiers (articles, adjectives, adverbs, and prepositional phrases) to find the N-V-N-N pattern. Beneath each sentence, write the subject (*n*), action verb (*av*), indirect object (*n*), and direct object (*n*) in order. Use your notes if you need help. The first one has been done for you.

           adj   pn   av   pn   adj   adj   n   pp   pn

Example: Black Americans gave America many great members (of Congress).

              Americans - gave - America - members

1) Blanche Kelso Bruce gave Missouri its first school for Black students in 1864.

2) In 1874, the Mississippi legislature gave Mr. Bruce the honor of the role of the state's first Black senator.

3) In 1888, Henry Plummer Cheatham gave North Carolina its first Black member of Congress.

4) After his defeat in 1892, Cheatham built North Carolina an orphanage for two hundred children.

5) Wood High School in Charleston, South Carolina, provided Robert Carlos DeLarge his early education.

7 Exercise A

6) In 1870, the South Carolina legislature <u>assigned</u> him the responsibility of land commissioner in charge of that state's public lands.

7) His success in that role provided <u>him</u> a nomination to the role of representative of the Second Congressional District.

8) In 1966, Massachusetts gave the United States its first <u>Black</u> senator from a popular election.

9) Senator Edward William Brooke III brought the people of Massachusetts twelve <u>years</u> of dedicated service in the Senate.

Exercise A 7

Directions
Write what job the underlined words are doing in each sentence. Choose your answers from among the following:

subject *direct object* *indirect object*
object of the preposition *verb* *modifier*

Sentence #	Word	Job
Ex.	members	*direct object*
1	Blanche Kelso Bruce	
3	Mr. Bruce	
4	Congress	
5	orphanage	
6	Robert Carlos DeLarge	
7	assigned	
8	him	
9	Black	
10	years	

7 EXERCISE B

Sentence Pattern 3: Exercise B

Directions

The sentences below are either Sentence Pattern 2 (N-V-N) or Pattern 3 (N-V-N-N). Parse the sentences and put the prepositional phrases in parentheses.

Then, on a separate piece of paper, diagram each sentence. Remember to strip each sentence of all modifiers (articles, adjectives, adverbs, and prepositional phrases) to find the sentence pattern. Use your notes if you need help.

1) Black Americans represent America in all aspects of our culture.

2) Mary McLeod Bethune gave the southeastern United States one of its finest teacher-training institutions.

3) The Brooklyn Dodgers gave Roy Campanella the "Most Valuable Player" award in three different years.

4) Wilt Chamberlain broke almost every scoring record in professional basketball.

5) In 1839, Joseph Cinque led a successful revolt against the captain of a slave ship.

6) Harriet Tubman gave many slaves their freedom through the famous Underground Railroad.

7) After his own escape to freedom in 1835, Frederick Douglass denounced slavery in his fiery speeches.

8) W.E.B. Dubois <u>founded</u> the National Association for the Advancement of Colored People.

9) James Baldwin gave the <u>world</u> such magnificent essays as "The Fire Next Time."

10) Lorraine Hansberry won the New York Drama Critics' Circle Award for <u>*A Raisin in the Sun*</u>.

Directions
Write what job the underlined words are doing in each sentence. Choose your answers from among the following:

subject   *direct object*   *indirect object*
object of the preposition   *verb*   *modifier*

Sentence #	Word	Job
1	America	
2	United States	
3	award	
4	every	
5	Joseph Cinque	
6	slaves	
7	slavery	
8	founded	
9	world	
10	*A Raisin in the Sun*	

7 EXERCISE C

Sentence Pattern 3: Exercise C

Directions

The sentences in this exercise are either Pattern 1 (N-V), Pattern 2 (N-V-N), or Pattern 3 (N-V-N-N). Parse each sentence and put parentheses around the prepositional phrases.

Then, on a separate piece of paper, diagram each sentence. Remember to strip each sentence of all modifiers to find the sentence pattern. Use your notes if you need help. Diagramming solutions are found after the index.

1) Langston Hughes achieved fame from his magnificent poems about the Black experience in America.

2) Langston Hughes made his entrance into the world in Joplin, Missouri, on February 1, 1902.

3) His father left the family for Mexico in a fit of rage over discrimination.

4) His mother gave her son the best home within her power.

5) His classmates in grammar school gave him the title of class poet.

6) On that same day, Hughes wrote sixteen verses in praise of them.

7) At his father's request, Hughes moved to Mexico in his junior year of high school.

8) He published his first poem during his senior year.

9) Hughes put himself through Lincoln College in Pennsylvania.

10) Throughout his long career, Langston Hughes gave America the priceless legacy of his poetry.

Directions
Write what job the underlined words are doing in each sentence. Choose your answers from among the following:

subject   *direct object*   *indirect object*
object of the preposition   *verb*   *modifier*

Sentence #	Word	Job
1	fame	
2	made	
3	rage	
4	son	
5	title	
7	Hughes	
8	poem	
10	America	
10	legacy	
10	poetry	

7 APPLICATION & ENRICHMENT

Application & Enrichment

Synonyms Activity 3

In the last Application & Enrichment, we looked at how using different, specific words when we write creates a more vivid word picture for readers. There's an easy way to take our descriptive writing up yet another notch! That's where modifiers—adjectives and adverbs—come in: they tell more about our nouns and verbs, clarifying even more the picture we are painting with words.

Let's look back at our previous, improved example sentence:

The vehicle drove on the road.

became

The bicycle wobbled along the trail.

We get a clearer picture of what's happening with these new, more specific synonyms in place. But we can make it even better by adding some modifiers. We know that adjectives describe nouns, so we can brainstorm some adjectives to describe *bicycle* and *trail*. Adverbs do the same thing for verbs (and other parts of speech), so let's come up with some for those, too. Have fun—visualize the effect you want to paint with your words. In our sentence, we want to suggest that the bicycle is neither new nor stable:

bicycle (adjectives)	ancient	decrepit	rusty	rickety
wobbled (adverbs)	uneasily	alarmingly	precariously	hazardously
trail (adjectives)	rocky	wooded	rugged	muddy

Choose your favorite from the sentences you created for the last Application & Enrichment in Lesson 6. Visualize the scene you are trying to describe. Then brainstorm four words each to describe the synonyms you put in your sentence that replaced the following:

_____ (adjectives) _____ _____ _____ _____
(vehicle)

_____ (adverbs) _____ _____ _____ _____
(drove)

_____ (adjectives) _____ _____ _____ _____
(road)

Now, plug these descriptors into your sentence. Here's our example sentence about the bicycle with the new modifiers we've chosen:

The ancient bicycle wobbled alarmingly along the rocky trail.

How much clearer and more vivid is that word picture? Remember that you can change the preposition if you need to, like we did! We also changed the order of the verb and adverb. It sounded better to us to say *wobbled alarmingly*, although *alarmingly wobbled* is also grammatically correct. You can do the same thing if you think it sounds better.

The _____ _____ _____ _____ on the _____ _____.
     (adj)   (vehicle)   (adv)   (drove)   (adj)   (road)

Sentence Pattern 3: Assessment

Directions
Parse the sentences below and put prepositional phrases in parentheses. Then, on a separate sheet of paper, diagram the sentences. Use your notes if you need any help.

1) Black Americans give the United States their gifts in all areas of American culture.

2) Black writers touch our hearts with their stories.

3) Black soldiers come to America's aid in times of war.

4) Show business in this country benefits from the talents of Black entertainers.

5) Black poets write us poems of great beauty.

6) The talents of great Black athletes enrich the sports scene in America.

7) American history contains the names of many Black patriots.

8) The ranks of Black Americans give us countless dedicated educators.

9) People of color contribute greatly to all walks of American life.

10) America prospers from the contributions of all her cultural groups.

7 Assessment

Directions
Write what job the underlined words are doing in each sentence. Choose your answers from among the following:

subject   *direct object*   *indirect object*
object of the preposition   *verb*   *modifier*

Sentence #	Word	Job
1	United States	
2	stories	
3	America's	
4	business	
5	us	
6	scene	
7	contains	
8	educators	
9	greatly	
10	groups	

Lesson 8
Linking Verbs and Sentence Patterns 4 & 5

Lesson 8: Linking Verbs and Sentence Patterns 4 & 5

We have learned three sentence patterns that all use action verbs. Now we will learn about a different kind of verb: the **linking verb**.

> **Linking verbs**
> A **linking verb** is a verb that establishes a connection between its subject and a complement in the **predicate**. The **complement** can be either a noun or pronoun that is another name for the subject, or it can be an adjective that describes the subject.

Here is the difference between action verbs and linking verbs:

James walked down the street.

The subject of this sentence is James. And James ***did*** something in the sentence: he walked.

Now, look at this sentence:

James seemed sleepy today.

The subject is still James, but James isn't ***doing*** anything in this sentence. Instead, he is ***being*** something: *sleepy.*

Always Linking Verbs	Sometimes Linking Verbs	
be (is, are, am, was were, being, been)	smell	stay
seem	taste	appear
become	look	sound
	feel	grow

Some of these verbs are always linking verbs, such as all forms of *be, seem* and *become*, but most of them can act as action verbs, too. All of the verbs that have to do with your senses can be linking verbs.

> **Tip:** There are a couple of ways to help you figure out if a verb is acting as a linking verb. The first is to substitute it with a form of *be*. If you can do that and the sentence still makes sense, it is almost definitely acting as a linking verb. Another way to check is to replace the verb with an equals sign. If you can do that, you know that the two nouns are "equals" and you have a linking verb!

Example A: Jasmine *feels* ill.   Jasmine *is* ill.

Poor Jasmine! This sentence still makes sense and means almost the same thing. *Feels* is doing the **linking verb** job.

Example B: Paolo *smells* dinner.   Paolo *is* dinner.

Oh dear, surely not! In this sentence, *smells* is doing the **action verb** job.

The test above works most of the time. To be absolutely sure it's a linking verb, though, you must determine if it's in a linking verb sentence pattern.

Sentence Pattern 4: N-LV-N

The first linking verb pattern is called "noun – linking verb – noun," or N-LV-N The first noun or pronoun is the **subject**. Next comes the **linking verb**, followed by the second noun, which is the **predicate nominative**. The most important thing to remember is that **the subject and predicate nominative are always the same person or thing.**

> **Predicate nominative**
> A **predicate nominative** is a noun or pronoun in the predicate that renames or restates the subject. It follows a **linking verb**.

                adj   n   lv art   n   pp art   pn

Example: My cousin is a captain (in the Navy).

Let's strip the sentence of modifiers and see what's left:

cousin – is – captain

Notice that *cousin* and *captain* are the same person in this sentence. If the sentence said, "My cousin *married* a captain in the Navy," that wouldn't be the case; the *cousin* and the *captain* are two different people. ***Married*** is an action verb and can only have direct and indirect objects. ***Is*** is a linking verb that links the predicate nominative back to the subject and can only have a complement.

Here's how we diagram Sentence Pattern 4:

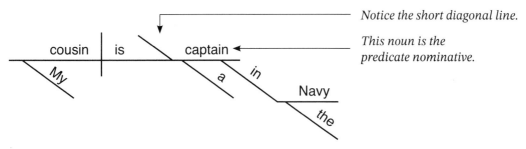

Notice the short diagonal line.

This noun is the predicate nominative.

Notice how the baseline is different from a Pattern 2 sentence with a direct object. You remember that the line separating an action verb from its direct object is vertical. In this pattern, however, the line separating the linking verb from the predicate nominative is diagonal, slanting back toward the subject.

> **Complement** comes from the same root word as **complete**. The predicate nominative or predicate adjective **completes** the subject by telling more about it.

Sentence Pattern 5: N-LV-ADJ

This is the second linking verb pattern, and the last of the five basic sentence patterns. It is called "noun – linking verb – adjective." This sentence pattern is similar to Pattern 4, except that instead of a predicate nominative (noun), there is a **predicate adjective** that describes the subject.

> **Predicate adjective**
> A **predicate adjective** is an adjective that follows a **linking verb** and describes the subject. It is a kind of complement.

Here's an example of a sentence with a predicate adjective:

    art   n   lv   adj   pp   art adj   n
    The students looked angry (about the pop quiz).

When we strip out all the modifiers, we are left with:

students – looked – angry

Using the questions from Step 2 of The Process Chart, we ask, "*which students*?" Who is *angry* describing? The answer is "*angry students*." Because **students** is the subject but **angry** is in the predicate, we know that **looked** is acting as a linking verb and **angry** is a **predicate adjective**.

Sentence Pattern 5 is diagrammed with the same diagonal line as Pattern 4:

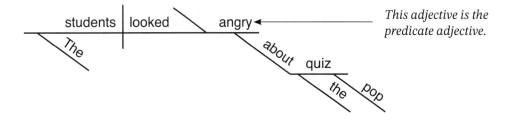

This adjective is the predicate adjective.

> We have already learned about the difference between **action verbs** (*av*) and **verbals** (*v*). Now we are adding **linking verbs** (*lv*).
>
> There's a reason that Step 5 asks you to simply mark everything that looks like a verb with a *v*. Steps 6-9 will help you to identify the main verb in the sentence as either an action verb or linking verb and add the appropriate tag. The questions asked in these steps will help you to identify the jobs of any nouns or adjectives in the predicate at the same time.
>
> Remember:
>
> - If you have an **action verb** in your sentence, then you have either Pattern 1, Pattern 2, or Pattern 3.
> - **Direct objects** and **indirect objects** must have an **action verb**.
> - If you have a **linking verb** in your sentence, then you have either Pattern 4 or Pattern 5.
> - **Predicate nominatives** or **predicate adjectives** must have a **linking verb**.

The Process

The Process Chart is now complete; there are no more steps to be added. If you follow the steps in order, you will find that The Process makes even complicated sentences easy!

Step 1. Find and mark all the nouns (***n***) and proper nouns (***pn***) in the sentence.
Step 2. Find and mark all the articles (***art***) and adjectives (***adj***) in the sentence.
Step 3. Find and mark all the pronouns (***pro***).
Step 4. Find and mark all the prepositions (***pp***). Put parentheses around all prepositional phrases.
Step 5. Find all words that look like verbs and mark them ***v***.
Step 6. Ask, "who or what (verb)?"

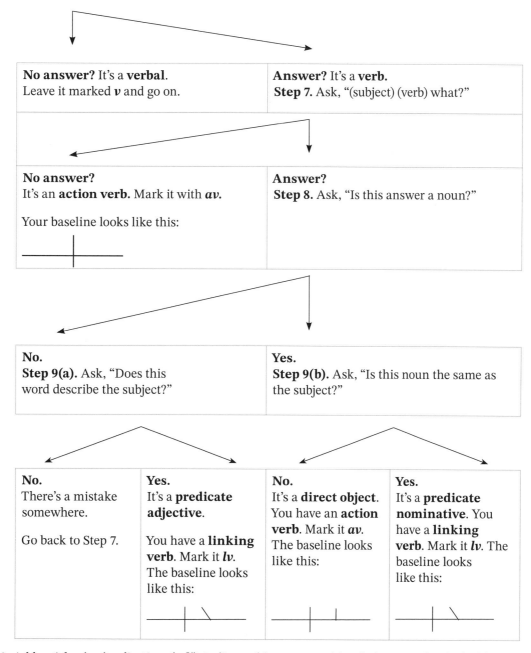

Step 10. Add articles (***art***), adjectives (***adj***), indirect objects, prepositional phrases, adverbs (***adv***), and conjunctions (***conj***)* to the diagram.

Step 11. Congratulate yourself! You've successfully parsed and diagrammed the whole sentence!

* Conjunctions are taught in Lesson 10. Don't worry about parsing or diagramming them until then.

8 EXERCISE A

Sentence Patterns 4 & 5: Exercise A

Directions

All of the sentences in this exercise are either Pattern 4 or Pattern 5; that is, they will have a linking verb and a complement, either a predicate nominative or a predicate adjective. Parse and then diagram each sentence. Use your Process Chart to work through the steps and figure out which pattern you have. Stripping the sentence of all modifiers can help you identify the parts of speech that will determine the pattern. Remember to use your notes and The Process Chart if you need any help.

1) Jewish Americans are important <u>contributors</u> to American culture.

2) George Burns was one of America's most beloved <u>comedians</u>.

3) The <u>extremely</u> talented Barbra Streisand is a famous popular singer.

4) Henry Kissinger <u>remained</u> America's powerful Secretary of State during the Nixon administration.

5) One influential Jewish-American publisher was <u>Joseph Pulitzer.</u>

6) Dr. Jonas Salk's polio <u>vaccine</u> was terribly important.

7) Albert Einstein's mind appeared more <u>brilliant</u> than any other.

8) The Baseball Hall of Fame's Sandy Koufax seemed greatly feared as a pitcher.

9) George Gershwin's music was incredibly beautiful.

10) The history of Jewish <u>Americans</u> is indeed remarkable.

Exercise A 8

Directions

Write which job the underlined word is doing in each sentence. Choose your answers from among the following:

subject	predicate nominative	predicate adjective
object of the preposition	modifier	verb

Sentence #	Word	Job
1	contributors	
2	comedians	
3	extremely	
4	remained	
5	Joseph Pulitzer	
6	vaccine	
7	brilliant	
10	Americans	

Sentence Patterns 4 & 5: Exercise B

Directions

All of the sentences in this exercise are either Pattern 4 or Pattern 5; that is, they will have a linking verb and a complement. Parse and then diagram each sentence. Use your Process Chart to work through the steps.

1) The young girl was terrified by the <u>guns</u> of the Nazi prison guards.

2) The members of her family became <u>prisoners</u> of the anti-Jewish German government in the early 1940s.

3) <u>Riva Minska</u> was a helpless inmate of Camp Mittelsteine in Germany.

4) The prisoner identification number on her arm was <u>55082</u>.

5) Riva <u>grew</u> weak from hunger.

6) This young girl felt desperately <u>lonely</u> for her parents.

7) They remained prisoners in a death camp in a <u>different</u> place.

8) The guards at Riva's <u>camp</u> were almost unbelievably cruel.

9) The mere idea of escape looked <u>hopeless</u>.

10) Riva <u>felt</u> less miserable in the secret world of her poetry.

Directions

Write what job the underlined words are doing in each sentence. Choose your answers from among the following:

subject *predicate nominative* *predicate adjective*
object of the preposition *modifier* *verb*

Sentence #	Word	Job
1	guns	
2	prisoners	
3	Riva Minska	
4	55082	
5	grew	
6	lonely	
7	different	
8	camp	
9	hopeless	
10	felt	

Sentence Patterns 4 & 5: Exercise C

Directions
The sentences below may be any one of the five sentence patterns you have learned: N-V, N-V-N, N-V-N-N, N-LV-N, and N-LV-ADJ. Use The Process Chart to parse and diagram each sentence.

1) The first group of Jews in America came from Brazil to New Amsterdam in 1654.

2) The second Jewish settlement in the American colonies was the village of Newport in Rhode Island in 1658.

3) Jews were "an alien nation," according to some ignorant settlers.

4) The first Jews in Pennsylvania traded with the Native Americans along the Delaware River in 1655.

5) The devout Jews of Philadelphia built themselves a very beautiful synagogue in 1770.

6) At the time of the American Revolution, approximately 2,500 Jews lived in the American colonies.

7) This tiny Jewish minority became historically important during the days of our fight for freedom from Great Britain.

8) Jews played an <u>important</u> part in the revolutionary struggle from the start.

9) Jews from Europe also joined in the fight for freedom.

10) Be <u>proud</u> of these early Jewish patriots!

Directions

Write what job the underlined words are doing in each sentence. Choose your answers from among the following:

subject   *direct object*   *indirect object*   *predicate nominative*

object of the preposition   *modifier*   *predictae adjective*   *verb*

Sentence #	Word	Job
1	came	
2	settlement	
2	village	
3	some	
4	first	
5	themselves	
5	synagogue	
7	minority	
8	important	
10	proud	

Application & Enrichment

Comma Splits

Commas are very important, often misunderstood punctuation marks. Using them correctly (or incorrectly!) makes a great difference in how easily your reader understands what you have written. You've learned a bit about fixing comma splices (in the Lesson 4 Application & Enrichment activity). Now you know enough grammar to learn about another common error that trips up readers.

We know that a comma means a pause in the flow of the text. When we see a comma, our mind naturally pauses in our reading. That's great when it's a properly placed comma, in a place where you want the reader to naturally pause. But when commas are in the wrong place, text lurches along like it is gasping for breath. Commas randomly placed in sentences are called **comma splits.**

Comma split

This is the opposite of a comma splice. Rather than incorrectly joining two sentences, a **comma split** incorrectly divides a sentence. It is a single comma that comes between two words, phrases, or clauses that shouldn't be separated. Here is a list of places a comma should never be:

1) There should never be **only one** comma between the **subject** and **verb**.

   Example:
   Incorrect: The butler carrying a tray, walked into the room.
   Correct: The butler, carrying a tray, walked into the room.
   Also correct: Carrying a tray, the butler walked into the room.

2) There should never be **only one** comma separating a **verb** and its **direct object**.

   Example:
   Incorrect: We discovered after searching carefully, many things.
   Correct: We discovered, after searching carefully, many things.
   Also correct: After searching carefully, we discovered many things.
   Or: We discovered many things after searching carefully.

3) There should never be **only one** comma separating a **linking verb** and its **predicate adjective** or **predicate nominative** (also known as its **complement**).

   Example:
   Incorrect: James felt, absolutely wonderful.
   Correct: James felt absolutely wonderful.

4) There should never be **only one** comma separating a **modifier** and its **noun**. If there is more than one adjective, there should be no comma after the final adjective before the noun.

   Example:
   Incorrect: The soft, cuddly, sweater was gorgeous.
   Correct: The soft, cuddly sweater was gorgeous.

5) There should never be **only one** comma separating a **verb** and its **indirect object**.

   Example:
   Incorrect: I wrote, my aunt in Florida a letter.
   Correct: I wrote my aunt in Florida a letter.

6) There should never be **only one** comma separating an **indirect object** and its **direct object**.

   Example:
   Incorrect: I wrote my aunt in Florida, a letter.
   Correct: I wrote my aunt in Florida a letter.

Always know **why** you are placing a comma in a sentence. Remember that nonessential information in the middle of a sentence needs to have commas on both ends. And remember the no-no splits!

1) **subject and verb**

2) **verb and direct object**

3) **linking verb and complement**

4) **modifier and its noun**

5) **verb and indirect object**

6) **indirect object and direct object**

Directions
The following sentences all contain comma splits. Using the list above, write what is being split by the comma.

Example: The football player, was tired from practice.

splits subject (player) and verb (was)

1) Joey threw him, the ball.

2) The orange, cat slept in the sun.

3) I read, my little cousin the book about dinosaurs.

4) Pudge Heffelfinger was, the first professional American football player.

5) The boy tossed, the ball back to the umpire.

Sentence Patterns 4 & 5: Assessment

Directions

The sentences below may be any one of the five sentence patterns you have learned. Use The Process Chart to parse and diagram each sentence.

1) Head coverings are a traditional symbol of modesty in Jewish culture.

2) In many orthodox Jewish communities, women wear head coverings in public after marriage.

3) Some Jewish women hide their own hair under a wig.

4) Others wear a knotted head scarf like other traditional Middle Eastern cultures.

5) These traditions go back thousands of years.

6) The traditional clothing of many cultures includes some kind of hair covering.

7) Scarves are a fashion choice for many wearers today.

8) The luxurious fabrics are beautifully embroidered with intricate patterns.

9) Layers of scarves provide people warmth in cold climates.

10) Head coverings <u>serve</u> many purposes in different communities around the world.

Directions

Write what job the underlined words are doing in each sentence. Choose your answers from among the following:

subject	*direct object*	*indirect object*	*predicate nominative*
object of the preposition	*modifier*	*predictae adjective*	*verb*

Sentence #	Word	Job
1	symbol	
2	women	
3	own	
4	cultures	
5	thousands	
6	kind	
7	choice	
8	embroidered	
9	people	
10	serve	

Lesson 9
Helping Verbs

Lesson 9: Helping Verbs

In this lesson, we will study **helping verbs**. To begin, we need to remember the definition of a **phrase**:

> **Phrases**
> A phrase is a group of words that works together as a unit to express a concept.

Helping verbs come before action verbs or linking verbs to create a **verb phrase**. They "help" by creating different tenses: past, future, conditional, and so on. In other programs, helping verbs are sometimes called auxiliary verbs. Using helping verbs changes what we know about the action of the main verb.

Example 1:　　Main verb　　　　crawl

　　　　　　　　Verb phrase　　　 will crawl　　　(*will* is the helping verb)

If we use this verb phrase in a sentence, what does it tell you about the action?

The baby will crawl.

Is the baby crawling right now? No. The baby will crawl at some point *in the future*.

Example 2:　　Main verb　　　　listen

　　　　　　　　Verb phrase　　　 has been listening　　(*has* and *been* are the helping verbs)

Here is the verb phrase in a sentence:

Juan has been listening to a lot of podcasts.

What do we know from this particular phrase? Juan started listening to podcasts at some point in the past, and he is still listening to a lot of podcasts. It shows a continuous, or **progressive**, action. If we took away the helping verbs, it would change the meaning slightly:

Juan listens to a lot of podcasts.

In this sentence, without the helping verbs, we know that Juan listens to podcasts, but we lose the fact that this is a change in his behavior—that he previously did not listen to podcasts, but at some point he started listening, and he still does. Without the helping verbs, we don't know as much about when Juan started listening.

> We'll talk more about how helping verbs create verb tenses in upcoming Application & Enrichment activities.

Example 3:   Main verb   find

   Verb phrase   would have been found   (*would, have,* and *been* are the helping verbs)

Let's use this verb phrase in a sentence:

The keys *would have been found*.

Have the keys been found? No. What word tells us that, specifically? **Would**. If we remove that word, the remaining helping verbs say the opposite. **Would** is an example of a **modal**, which is a helping verb that makes the action or linking verb **conditional**. That means that the action of the main verb is not a done deal—it is only hypothetical. Something else would need to happen before the action becomes reality. In our example sentence, we can add a condition to the end to illustrate this:

The keys would have been found *if we had looked under the mat*.

If we had looked under the mat...did we look under the mat? No, but *if* we **had**, we would have found the keys. That's the condition that is implied by using **would** in this sentence.

So you can see that using helping verbs adds a whole range of meaning to our sentences beyond what a simple action or linking verb can provide!

Here is a list of verbs that can do the helping verb job. You should become very familiar with these verbs:

to be:	to have:	The Modals
is	has	will
am	have	would
are	had	shall
was		should
were	**to do:**	can
be	do	could
being	does	may
been	did	might
		must

You'll notice that some of the verbs listed as sometimes helping verbs can also be **action verbs,** such as *have* and *do*. If one of these verbs is the *last* verb in a verb phrase, it is doing the job of an **action verb.** If it is *not* the last verb in a verb phrase, it is doing the job of a **helping verb.**

9 Student Notes

                pro hv av adj   n

Example 4:   I will do my homework.   (*will do* is the verb phrase and *do* is an action verb)

                pro hv adv   av   adj   n

                I do not* want any lunch.   (*do want* is the verb phrase and *do* is a helping verb)

*****Not*** is always an adverb that negates, or flips, the verb to mean the opposite.

There are also verbs on the helping verbs list above that you have learned as linking verbs (all the forms of the verb **to be**). If they are the *last* verb in the verb phrase, they are doing the job of a **linking verb**. If they are anywhere else in the verb phrase, they are doing the job of a **helping verb**.

                pn   hv lv art   n

Example 5:   John will be* a senior.   (*will be* is the verb phrase and *be* is a linking verb)

                pn   hv   av   pp   n

                John is going (to college).   (*is going* is the verb phrase and *is* (a form of *to be*) is a helping verb)

*****Be*** is always the form of ***to be*** that's used as a linking verb if there is a helping verb, no matter what the subject is.

> Note: A favorite spot for adverbs to hide is between a helping verb and the main verb (*I should **really** do my homework*). That's why it's so useful to be familiar with the helping verbs—otherwise, you might mistake an adverb for a helping verb or vice versa.

How to diagram helping verbs

Helping verbs are just part of the verb phrase, so they are diagrammed together with the main verb like this:

                pn   hv   lv adj   adj   n   pp   adj   n

Example 6:   Josephine will be my study partner (in algebra class).

```
Josephine | will be \ partner
                my \ study \ in \ class
                                     \ algebra
```

How to diagram questions

Most of the questions in English are formed by rearranging the words in a statement and putting them in a different order. Look at the following examples:

Example 7:   **Statement:**   I should do my homework.

   Question: Should I do my homework?

To form the question, the helping verb is moved in front of the subject. To diagram a question, the helping verb(s) and main verb still go in the verb position. The first word of the sentence should be capitalized to show that it came first in the sentence.

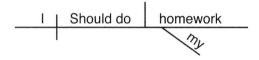

Example 8:   **Statement:**   He walked to school.

   Question: Did he walk to school?

In Example 8, because there was no helping verb in the statement, one was added to make the question. But again, it comes in front of the subject.

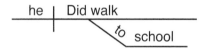

Helping Verbs: Exercise A

Directions
Parse and diagram the sentences. Be on the lookout for adverbs hiding inside verb phrases! Use The Process Chart and your notes for help. Diagramming solutions are found after the index.

1) Santha Rama Rau was born in India in 1923.

2) Rama Rau has long been famous for her superb essays.

3) She could have been well known for her writings beyond her essays.

4) She could easily have been popular for her novels, also.

5) In "By Any Other Name," she has portrayed the cultural conflict in India because of the English colonization.

6) Do you know anything about cultural conflicts?

7) This essay might help you to an understanding of such conflicts.

8) Two Indian sisters were sent to a school for English children.

9) The Anglo-Indian school had been taught by British teachers for years.

10) This British-run school must have caused many cultural problems for its Indian students.

9 EXERCISE B

Helping Verbs: Exercise B

Directions
Parse and diagram the sentences below. Look out for adverbs. Use The Process Chart and your notes if you need help. Diagramming solutions are found after the index.

1) The sisters had been given two beautiful Indian names by their parents.

2) On the first day of school, the teacher had indicated her helplessness with Indian names.

3) Santha's new name would be Cynthia.

4) Premila would be known as Pamela.

5) The girls could not understand the reason for these new names.

6) They would soon understand the reasons for their mother's anxiety about this new English school.

7) Four other Indian children had been assigned to the same class with the two sisters.

8) One of the other girls was wearing a cotton dress instead of her native Indian clothes.

9) The girls <u>would ask</u> their mother about the possibility of English-style dresses

for themselves.

10) Did <u>they</u> have a good reason for their desire for different clothes?

Fill in the blank

11) Helping verbs are verbs that come _____ the main verb and help form different _____ .

12) Adjectives are words that _____ .

13) A pronoun is a word that _____ .

14) The helping verb(s) and the main verb together make up the _____ .

9 EXERCISE B

Directions
Write what job the underlined word is doing in each sentence. Choose your answers from among the following:

subject	*direct object*	*object of the preposition*	*verb*
indirect object	*predicate nominative*	*predicate adjective*	*modifier*

Sentence #	Word	Job
1	Indian	
2	teacher	
3	Cynthia	
4	Pamela	
5	new	
6	reasons	
7	Four	
8	clothes	
9	would ask	
10	They	

Helping Verbs: Exercise C

Directions
Parse and diagram the sentences below. Diagramming solutions are found after the index.

1) That first <u>day</u> of school had been very difficult for the two sisters.

2) Santha <u>had been asked</u> by the teacher for her new name.

3) She could not remember <u>it</u>!

4) The rest of the <u>class</u> had laughed at her.

5) She had been a very embarrassed <u>girl</u>!

6) At <u>lunchtime</u>, the other Indian students were eating sandwiches instead of normal Indian food.

7) At recess, she could not understand the competitive <u>games.</u>

8) At home, the <u>girls</u> had been taught kindness to younger children in their games.

9) These English children did not return the <u>same</u> courtesy!

9 EXERCISE C

10) The two sisters would feel <u>glad</u> at the close of school on that first day.

Fill in the blank

11) An antecedent is_____.

12) In a *noun – linking verb – noun* sentence pattern, the second noun is called the_____.

13) List the modifiers in this sentence. _____

14) The verb phrase is made up of the _____.

Directions

Write what job each underlined word is doing in the sentence. Choose your answers from among the following:

subject　　　*direct object*　　　*object of the preposition*　　　*verb*
indirect object　　*predicate nominative*　　*predicate adjective*　　*modifier*

Sentence #	Word	Job
1	day	
2	had been asked	
3	it	
4	class	
5	girl	
6	lunchtime	
7	games	
8	girls	
9	same	
10	glad	

Application & Enrichment

Synonyms Activity 4

We've described synonyms and modifiers as adding "spice and flavor" to our writing. But, just like eating too much ice cream can give you a stomach ache, too many synonyms, adjectives, or adverbs can detract from your message. Readers can get lost trying to follow your words if there are too many or they're too complicated.

So how much description is enough? That's a matter of personal preference, as a writer, but there are some guidelines you can follow to help you decide.

1) Use synonyms that your reader will understand.

   The secondary interlocutor impeded evolution of our colloquy to achieve congruity.

   Huh? This sentence is packed with fancy synonyms, but it doesn't make much sense!

   Try this one:
   The other speaker stopped the progress of our conversation toward agreement.

   Now we can understand it, but it's still a little awkward. Let's think about what we're trying to say and try again:

   The other speaker stopped us from reaching an agreement.

   Much better and clearer! Good writing should not be complicated or confusing. We need to take care not to use fancy words just because we can. Every word we choose needs to have a purpose in our sentence.

2) Coco Chanel, known as one of the most elegant women who ever lived, gave the following advice about jewelry: "Before leaving the house, look in the mirror and take one thing off." This is great advice when we look at our descriptive sentences, too. Are all of the synonyms we are using adding to the word picture we want to paint? What about the modifiers we've added—are they all essential to the picture? Are there any repetitive words that can be removed? Look closely at your sentence. Is there anything you can take off without losing the meaning?

   Here's a puffed-up sentence with lots of descriptors:

   The wizened, bent, unkempt, messy old woman happily, peacefully lived with her bony, skinny, toothless cat in her small, tiny, cramped, cozy cottage.

   If we look at each noun and adjective with its modifiers, there are some words with very similar meanings that can be eliminated. Let's look at the first noun phrase:

   The wizened, bent, unkempt, messy old woman

   Wizened and *bent* mean almost the same thing; choose one to keep. The same is true of *unkempt* and *messy*; again, choose just one. *Old*, however, is on its own, and none of our other modifiers say that, so we should keep it. Write your new noun phrase on the line below:

   _____

Next we have a verb phrase with some adverbs:
happily, peacefully lived

While *happily* and *peacefully* don't mean the same thing, they don't really add a lot to the sentence together. We would get the same mental image with only one or the other. Choose one of the adverbs to keep, and write your new verb phrase below:

_____

Look at the next noun phrase: *bony, skinny, toothless cat.* What can you take out of the phrase but still paint the proper mental picture?

_____

Now do the same with the last noun phrase: *small, tiny, cramped, cozy cottage*

_____

Finally, put it all together by writing the simplified sentence with your new phrases below:

_____

Your new and improved sentence should be much clearer and easier to read while losing none of the "spice and flavor" synonyms and modifiers provide.

Helping Verbs: Assessment

Directions
Parse and diagram all of the sentences below.

1) On the day of Premila's first test, the girls' lives would change in a big way.

2) Premila had suddenly marched through the door of Santha's classroom.

3) "We are leaving this place now!"

4) Santha had been completely dumbfounded by Premila's behavior.

5) She could not disobey her sister, however.

6) "I can never attend that school again."

7) On the way to their home, Santha was wondering about the reason for their sudden departure.

8) At home, Mother would ask for a reason.

9) The British teacher had accused all the Indian students of cheating on tests!

10) To happy little Santha, however, this bad thing had happened to a girl by the name of Cynthia!

Fill in the blank

11) A helping verb helps the main verb form different _____.

12) A verb is not a verb unless it has a _____.

13) Which word in this sentence is the predicate nominative? _____.

14) An adjective is a word that _____.

15) A pronoun is a word that _____.

16) What is an antecedent? _____.

17) Which kind of noun can consist of more than one word? _____.

18) The helping verb(s) and the main verb make up the _____.

9 Assessment

Directions
Write what job the underlined words are doing in each sentence. Choose your answers from among the following:

subject   *direct object*   *object of the preposition*   *verb*
indirect object   *predicate nominative*   *predicate adjective*   *modifier*

Sentence #	Word	Job
1	lives	
2	door	
3	are leaving	
4	dumbfounded	
5	sister	
6	that	
7	departure	
8	Mother	
9	had accused	
10	Cynthia	

Lesson 10
Conjunctions & Compound Situations

Lesson 10: Conjunctions & Compound Situations

In this lesson, we will learn about small, simple words we use every day. They're called **conjunctions**. We use them to join together words, phrases, and sentences, and they can change the meaning of what we say. Look at these sentences:

You can invite Phoebe, Sanjay, *and* Rob to the movies with you. (Three people are going to the movies with you.)

You can invite Phoebe, Sanjay, *or* Rob to the movies with you. (One person is going to the movies with you.)

What a difference can be made by changing just one little word!

> **Conjunctions**
> A conjunction is a word that joins **grammatical equals**: a noun to a noun, a verb to a verb, a phrase to a phrase, or even a sentence to a sentence.

The two (or more) things that are being joined together by the conjunction **must be the same kind of thing!**

There are three kinds of conjunctions:

- Coordinating conjunctions
- Correlative conjunctions
- Subordinating conjunctions (we'll talk about these in Level 4)

Coordinating conjunctions

A coordinating conjunction is a word that connects two or more words, sentences, phrases, or clauses. Remember, whatever items are being joined by a coordinating conjunction must be the same part of speech!

for (*when it means **because***)*

and

nor

but

or

yet (*when it means **but***)*

so

And is the most commonly used conjunction, so it's the one in most of the examples and exercises. You can remember all of these conjunctions with the acronym FANBOYS, which uses the first letter of each one.

*In today's English, *for* is usually a preposition and *yet* is usually an adverb, but if you read older or more advanced literature, you may see these words doing their conjunction jobs.

	pn	av	art	n	conj	art	n

Example 1:   Anne cleaned the kitchen and the bedroom.

And joins two nouns: *kitchen* and *bedroom*.

	pro	hv	av	pp	art	n	conj	pp	art	n

Example 2:   We will go (to the store) and (to the cleaners).

And joins two prepositional phrases: *to the store* and *to the cleaners*.

Correlative conjunctions

Correlative conjunctions do the same job as coordinating conjunctions: they connect grammatical equals, whether words, phrases, or sentences. However, they will always be found in pairs with other words between.

either...or   both...and

neither...nor   not only...but (also)*

*Sometimes *also* will not be in the sentence, but it's always implied.

	pro	hv	av		art	n		art	n

Example 3:   You can take either the pie or the cake.

conj

(Notice how correlative conjunctions are parsed: underline them and draw an arrow to each; mark **conj** beneath the sentence.)

Either...or joins two nouns: *pie* and *cake*.

	art	n	lv		adj		adj

Example 4:   The cat is both beautiful and smart.

conj

Both...and joins two predicate adjectives: *beautiful* and *smart*.

Now you try. What are the correlative conjunctions in the following sentences? What parts of speech do they connect?

My cat Pumpkin is not only orange but also round.

Neither diet nor exercise is able to help her.

Compound Situations

A **compound situation** is when there are two (or more) of something joined by a conjunction in a sentence. All sentences that have any kind of a conjunction include a compound situation. Two or more subjects joined by a conjunction is called a **compound subject**, two or more verbs joined by a conjunction is a **compound verb**, and so on, all the way up to a **compound sentence**.

To diagram a compound situation, go to the place where that word, if it were only one word, would be diagrammed. Then you will make "branches" to add as many words or phrases as necessary. The conjunction is added on a dotted line that connects the parts of the compound situation, just like a conjunction does in a sentence. Compare the following examples:

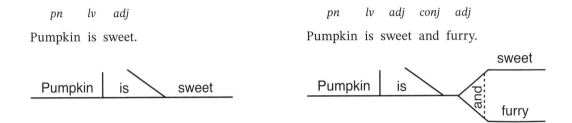

As you know, a predicate adjective is diagrammed by marking a diagonal line on the baseline between the linking verb and the predicate adjective. In the second sentence, the line branches after the diagonal because there are two predicate adjectives that both describe Pumpkin the cat.

All of the possible compound situations you might come across have been diagrammed on the following pages.

A) Compound Subject

            pn   conj   pn   av   adv

Example: Adam and Emma walked home.

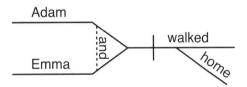

B) Compound Verb

           pn   hv   av   conj   av   art   n

Example 1:   John was washing and waxing the car.

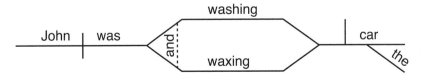

Notice that the baseline branches after *was* (which applies to both verbs) and is rejoined before the direct object *car* (which is the direct object of both verbs). Only the parts that are compounds need to be branched.

       pn av art n conj av art n

Example 2: John washed the car and mowed the lawn.

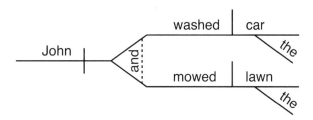

In this example, the baseline branches before the verb and does not need to be rejoined, because each verb has its own direct object, and there was nothing shared in the rest of the predicate.

C) Compound Direct Object

       pn av art   n conj art adj   n

Example: Olivia cleaned the kitchen and the living room.

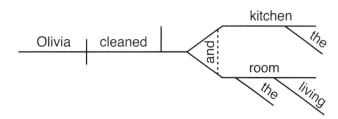

D) Compound Indirect Object

     ——pn—— av adj   n   conj pro art   n

Example: Aunt Mia sent my brother and me a present.

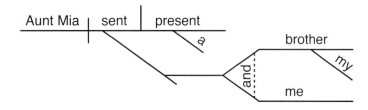

E) Compound Predicate Nominative or Predicate Adjective

       pro lv   adj conj adj

Example: She felt hungry and tired.

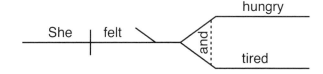

F) Compound Prepositional Phrases

Example:
    pro av pp art n conj pp art n
    We rode (over the river) and (through the woods).

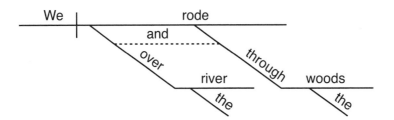

G) Prepositional Phrase with Compound Object

Example:
    pro av pp art adj n conj n
    She dusted (under the new table and chairs).

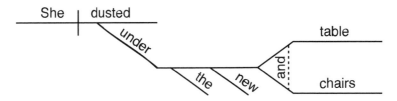

Notice that *the* and *new* are diagrammed on the line before the branch. These words modify both *table* and *chairs,* so they are not part of the branch.

H) Compound Sentence

Example:
    pn av art n conj pn av pro
    Jen washed the car and Jim waxed it.

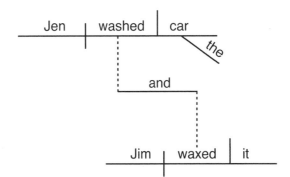

I) Multiple Compound Situations

Example:
    pn conj pn   av   conj   av   art   n
    Jen and Jim washed and waxed the car.

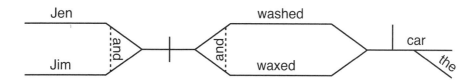

J) Diagramming Correlative Conjunctions

Example:
    pn   pn   av adj   n   adv
    Both Sean and Jason left their bikes outside.
    ←—conj—→

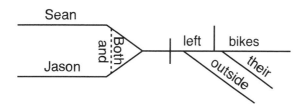

K) Compound Modifiers

Example:
    adj adj conj adj   n   av
    My black and white dog barked.

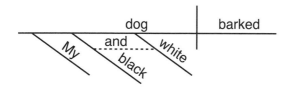

L. Three or More of Something

Example:
    pn pn conj pn av   n
    John, Joe, and Jim ate lunch.

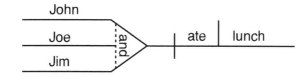

Conjunctions & Compound Situations: Exercise A

Directions
Parse and diagram the sentences below. Use the hints provided in the lesson notes to see how each compound should be diagrammed.

1) Fairy tales and nursery rhymes entertain most young children.
   (See Notes A)

2) Our parents either read or tell us these favorite stories.

   (See Notes B Example 1 and J)

3) Our first teachers tell the stories and sing the nursery rhymes with us.
   (See Notes B Example 2)

4) I loved nursery rhymes and fairy tales.
   (See Notes C)

5) My mother would read my brothers and me stories before bedtime.
   (See Notes D)

6) We were always quiet and spellbound.
   (See Notes E)

7) She would read them either in the living room or in our bedrooms.

   (See Notes F and J)

8) She had special voices for the animals and characters in the stories.
(See Notes G)

9) I loved "Little Red Riding Hood" and my brothers loved "Pinocchio."
(See Notes H)

10) Billy, George, and I were always perfect children during story time!
(See Notes L)

10 EXERCISE B

Conjunctions & Compound Situations: Exercise B

Directions
Parse and diagram each sentence. Use The Process Chart and your lesson notes if you need help.

1) Little Red Riding Hood and her mother packed a basket with cookies for her grandma.

2) The path to Grandma's house went through the forest and up the hill.

3) Little Red Riding Hood ran and skipped down the forest path.

4) The Big Bad Wolf waited behind a tree, and Little Red Riding Hood skipped past.

5) The Big Bad Wolf jumped from the bushes and in front of Little Red Riding Hood.

6) The wolf asked Little Red Riding Hood the purpose and destination of her journey.

7) "I am going to my grandma's, and I am not afraid of you!"

8) Little Red Riding Hood grabbed her basket and continued her journey.

9) Her grandma looked both big and strange to her.

10) The Big Bad Wolf jumped at Little Red Riding Hood and frightened her badly.

Fill in the blank

11) Two or more subjects in a sentence is called a _____.

12) When the noun before the verb means the same thing as the noun after the verb, the kind of verb you have is _____.

13) An adverb can modify _____, _____, or _____.

Conjunctions & Compound Situations: Exercise C

Directions
Parse and diagram each sentence. Use The Process Chart and your lesson notes if you need help.

1) Not only fairy tales but also nursery rhymes teach children values and lessons.

2) Many beloved European tales were written by Hans Christian Andersen and the Brothers Grimm.

3) Hans Christian Andersen wrote "The Ugly Duckling" and "The Little Mermaid."

4) The Brothers Grimm gave us "Little Red Riding Hood" and "Hansel and Gretel."

5) Hans Christian Andersen was born in Denmark, and the Brothers Grimm were born in Germany

6) These fairy tales and nursery rhymes are examples of the strong European influence in our country's culture.

7) Many of our fairy tales come from Europe, but children's stories are told in all countries and in all cultures.

8) Other <u>popular</u> stories come from China, India, Africa, and the Middle East.

9) <u>Interestingly</u>, all of them teach the same values and lessons to children.

10) These human values are <u>common</u> to cultures far and wide.

Fill in the blank

11) A noun is a word that _____.

12) The articles in English are _____.

13) An antecedent is _____.

14) In a *noun-linking verb-adjective* pattern, the adjective is called the _____.

15) List three jobs that a noun can do:

   _____,

   _____,

   or _____.

10 EXERCISE C

Directions

Write what jobs the underlined words are doing in each sentence. Choose your answer from among the following:

subject   *object of the preposition*   *verb*
modifier   *direct object*   *indirect object*
predicate nominative   *predicate adjective*

Sentence #	Word	Job
1	children	
2	tales	
3	wrote	
4	"Hansel and Gretel"	
5	Denmark	
6	examples	
7	Many	
8	popular	
9	Interestingly	
10	common	

Application & Enrichment

Starting a Sentence with a Conjunction

Sometimes grammar rules that had been taught in the past are now outdated. Others are just plain wrong! So let's just ignore them all, right? Well, no, it's not that easy. There are many people who have learned the old incorrect or outdated rules. The problem is that these people may be potential employers, your college professors, or other people who have authority to make judgments about you in some way. If your grammar is wrong in their eyes, then it might as well be wrong. They will probably judge your writing by the rules they believe to be correct.

That's why, sometimes, you will need to stick to these outdated rules when a situation calls for "formal writing." This is the kind of writing that is expected when communicating with and within most schools, industries, and businesses. For example, academics and scientists almost always use formal writing for their research papers, articles, and dissertations. College professors often look for formal language in papers for their classes. The grammar of formal writing changes much more slowly than informal writing or language, and these old rules still apply. Think of following these outdated rules as one way that you need to change your writing for a particular audience or situation.

One of the grammar "rules" that many people believe but that is actually incorrect is this:

Do not start a sentence with a conjunction!

Some people have been taught that it creates a sentence fragment. But it doesn't; not automatically, anyway. As long as the conjunction is followed by a complete sentence, it's grammatically correct to begin a sentence with one!

Subordinate and correlative conjunctions frequently start sentences.

Example: *Because* there was nothing good on TV, **I read my book for a while**.

Because is the subordinate conjunction, but it doesn't come immediately before the complete sentence *I read my book for a while*. The complete sentence doesn't need to immediately follow the conjunction.

Example: *Either* he goes *or* I go!

In this case, there's a complete sentence following each part of the conjunction.

That leaves coordinating conjunctions, such as **and**, **but**, and **or** (and the others listed in the notes for this lesson). The rule against starting a sentence with one of them may be outdated. But there are two rules to follow if you want to try it.

1) The sentence needs to relate to the information before it. Conjunctions join things that are equal or relate them in some way. Even at the beginning of a sentence, they still do the same job.

2) There must be an independent clause following the coordinating conjunction—no sentence fragments! It doesn't need to immediately follow the conjunction, but it needs to be somewhere in the sentence.

Example: Many people enjoy cilantro in their salsa and find it delicious. But others think it tastes like soap and recoil in disgust.

1) Sentence 2 relates to Sentence 1. Both sentences are talking about cilantro in salsa. Sentence 2 uses *But* to show that it contains information that contrasts with Sentence 1. (Think about what the conjunctions mean; see this lesson's notes for more information.)

2) Sentence 2 contains an independent clause (or complete sentence). It has a subject (*others*) and a verb (actually, two: *think* and *recoil*).

Starting a sentence with a conjunction can be used to:

- add emphasis or impact

    I won the baking contest. And I've only been baking for eight months!
    (*compare this to using a comma:* I won the baking contest, and I've only been baking for eight months! *It still means the same thing, but the added emphasis on the short time that I've been baking is lost.*)

- imitate the natural flow of conversation

    "Hi, Mary! It's been a while. So how have you been?"

Be careful not to overdo it, or it can lose its effectiveness. If you have multiple sentences in a row beginning with conjunctions, it can seem very choppy to readers. This passage is grammatically correct, but it leaves you almost breathless after reading it:

So it's almost Christmas. And I was thinking about what to get for Mom. But I don't have a lot of money. So I tried to think of something I could give her for free. And I thought maybe I could clean the entire house for her. Or maybe I could do the laundry every week. But I'm still not sure what to give her. Nor* do I have much time left!

*When using *nor* in a sentence, the subject and verb invert to question format. Notice that the verb, *do*, comes before the subject, *I*.

Directions

Read the following pairs of sentences. Add a conjunction to the beginning of the second sentence that shows the relationship between the sentences. Use one of the FANBOYS coordinating conjunctions—*for, and, nor, but, or, yet,* or *so*—and choose the one that emphasizes the relationship.

Example: I can't wait to see the article about our fundraiser.
<u>But (or Yet)</u> the newspaper delivery is late today.

These conjunctions show the contrast between the two sentences. Yet *can be used anywhere that you would use* but. *Because* yet *isn't commonly used as a conjunction in modern English, it sounds more formal to the reader or listener.*

1) We were hoping that the kitchen renovation would be completed by now. _____ it is not.

2) The game came down to a 48-yard field goal with no time left on the clock. _____ the kicker made it!

3) If Mia wants to go to the play with us, she needs to be here by 6:30. _____ she can stay home if she prefers. _____ I hope she decides to come with us!

4) No one has asked for my opinion of the new couch. _____ will I give it!

Directions

Each of the following begins with a conjunction. If the conjunction is followed by a complete sentence, write *sentence* in the blank. If it is followed by a sentence fragment, write *fragment*.

5) And your little dog, too! _____

6) But that's just how it goes sometimes. _____

7) Or we could always help at a soup kitchen for Thanksgiving. _____

8) For amber waves of grain. _____

9) Yet another reality television show. _____

10 ASSESSMENT

Conjunctions & Compound Situations: Assessment

Directions

Parse and diagram the sentences below. Use The Process Chart and your notes if you need help.

1) <u>Parents</u> should read fairy tales and nursery rhymes to their <u>children</u>.

2) Not only do children love these <u>stories</u>, but they learn many valuable lessons, too.

3) "The Ugly Duckling" can teach <u>children</u> kindness and tolerance of others' differences.

4) Cinderella was always <u>good</u> and patient, and she was rewarded in the end.

5) Two little pigs <u>built</u> their houses of straw and wood, but the third pig built his house of brick.

6) Good planning and hard work saved all three little <u>pigs'</u> lives.

7) Snow White helped the dwarfs and escaped the evil queen's plot at the same <u>time</u>.

8) Pinocchio's lies and stories led him <u>away</u> from his father and lengthened his nose!

9) "The Emperor's New Clothes" is a story about the dangers of dishonesty and false pride.

10) <u>We</u> learn many valuable life lessons in our childhood stories and rhymes.

Directions

Write what job the underlined words is doing in each sentence. Choose your answer from among the following:

subject   *object of the preposition*   *verb*
modifier   *direct object*   *indirect object*
predicate nominative   *predicate adjective*

Sentence #	Word	Job
1	Parents	
1	children	
2	stories	
3	children	
4	good	
5	built	
6	pigs'	
7	time	
8	away	
10	We	

10 Assessment

Fill in the blank

11) A noun is a word that _____.

12) The articles in English are _____.

13) An adjective is a word that _____.

14) A pronoun is a word that _____.

15) An antecedent is _____.

16) A verb isn't a "real" verb unless it has a _____.

17) True or false: A direct object occurs with a linking verb. _____

18) In a N-LV-N sentence, the second noun is called the _____.

19) An adverb is a word that _____.

20) The job that prepositional phrases do is _____.

21) A word can't be a preposition unless it's in a _____.

22) Two or more subjects in a sentence is called a _____.

23) The helping verb(s) and the main verb make up the _____.

24) Write an example of a correlative conjunction: _____.

25) The adjective following a linking verb is called the: _____.

Congratulations!

You've completed ANALYTICAL GRAMMAR Level 3: Parts of Speech

You are ready to continue the course in Level 4: Phrases and Clauses

Taking a break between levels?
Complete one Reinforcement exercise
every two weeks and you will
keep your skills sharp and ready!

Level 3
Reinforcing Skills

Congratulations on completing Level 3! At this point, it is important to reinforce the parsing and diagramming skills you learned in these lessons so they aren't forgotten. You will use these grammar skills as you learn more complex grammar components in Level 4.

This book has 18 reinforcement exercises and answer keys that will keep your parsing, diagramming, and paraphrasing skills sharp. These exercises include material from a wide variety of books, poems, and stories. While completing these exercises, you might find something you would love to read!

You should complete, then correct, each exercise on your own. Remember to use The Process Chart and the notes if you need help. If these skills are reinforced periodically, you will be well-prepared when it's time to start Level 4.

Exercise 1: *The Wind in the Willows* by Kenneth Grahame

This exercise is taken from a book which tells of the adventures of Badger, Rat, Mole, and Mr. Toad, who all live by the riverbank.

Parse the following sentences from the book:

1) The Rat said nothing, but stopped and unfastened a rope and hauled on it; he lightly stepped into a little boat which the Mole had not observed.

2) Toad found himself in a dank and noisome dungeon, and knew that all the grim darkness of a medieval fortress lay between him and the outer world of sunshine and highroads.

Paraphrase the following from *The Wind in the Willows*:
Write your answer on a separate piece of paper.

3) The following evening the Mole, who had risen late and taken things very easy all day, was sitting on the bank fishing, when the Rat, who had been looking up his friends and gossiping, came strolling along to find him. "Heard the news?" he said. "There's nothing else being talked about, all along the river bank. Toad went up to Town by an early train this morning. And he has ordered a large and very expensive motorcar."

Exercise: 1 Reinforcement

Parse and diagram the following sentences:

4) Mr. Toad was a very enthusiastic creature, and he was always getting bright ideas.

5) His enthusiasms often pitchforked him into trouble.

6) Toad saw a shiny new motorcar, and he wanted one immediately.

7) Driving was not his best accomplishment, and he crashed into all sorts of things.

8) Toad's animal friends on the riverbank kept Toad in his house until the end of this fad.

Exercise 2: *National Velvet* by Enid Bagnold

This is the story of a horse-mad young girl who is given a pony which she trains for the Grand National, the greatest horse race in England.

Parse the following sentences from the book:

1) Velvet produced a piece of sugar and the pony bent her head round with a look of insolence.

2) In the one local paper which they took there was a lot about Velvet, but no one thought to send out for all the other papers.

Paraphrase the following from *National Velvet*:

Write your answer on a seperate piece of paper.

3) "Stop! Stand! He's never going over that!"

> The ground had dropped away so sharply at the far corner that the original builder of the cobbled wall, to keep his coping straight, had heightened the wall itself. It was five feet two at the end of the field, with a fine downhill take-off. The horse sailed over like a dappled flying boat. It was a double spring. As he was high in the air he saw also to his hind feet and drew them up sharply.

> "...AND to spare," said Mi quietly, nodding his head. "A horse like that'd win the National."

Exercise: 2 Reinforcement

Parse and diagram the following sentences:

4) Velvet loved horses with all her heart and desperately wanted one of her own.

5) On the day of the village fair, Velvet won a horse in a raffle.

6) This horse would jump over tall fences and run madly through the town.

7) Velvet's secret dream was first prize in the Grand National.

8) The story of Velvet and her astonishing horse is one of the best-loved stories of all time.

Exercise 3: *Holes* by Louis Sachar

This book is about a boy named Stanley who is falsely accused of a crime and sent to a detention camp. There are some strange things going on at Camp Green Lake!

Parse the following sentences from the book:

1) Everyone in his family had always liked the fact that "Stanley Yelnats" was spelled the same frontward and backward.

2) Stanley and his parents didn't believe in curses, of course, but whenever anything went wrong, it felt good to be able to blame someone.

When parsing or diagramming a contraction, you must break it into its separate words and identify each part. The word *didn't* is a combination of *did* and *not*. The apostrophe represents a missing letter, and the two words have been combined into one. So in this example, *didn't* would be parsed as *hv/adv*, because *did* is doing the job of a helping verb, while *n(o)t* is an adverb.

Paraphrase the following from *Holes*:

Write your answer on a seperate piece of paper.

3) There is no lake at Camp Green Lake. There once was a very large lake here, the largest lake in Texas. That was over a hundred years ago. Now it is just a dry, flat wasteland.

   There used to be a town of Green Lake as well. The town shriveled and dried up along with the lake, and the people who lived there.

   During the summer the daytime temperature hovers around ninety-five degrees in the shade—if you can find any shade. There's not much shade in a big dry lake.

Exercise: 3 Reinforcement

Parse and diagram the following sentences:

4) Stanley Yelnats is a boy from a poor family with nothing but bad luck.

5) He is falsely accused of a crime and sent to Camp Green Lake in the arid Texas desert.

6) The boys at the camp must dig a deep hole daily, or they will be harshly punished.

7) The Warden rewards them for the discovery of "interesting" things, and soon Stanley becomes suspicious.

8) Anything could be hidden in the dried-up bed of Green Lake!

Exercise 4: *Where the Sidewalk Ends* by Shel Silverstein

This exercise is from a book of poems for children and young people. These two sentences are from the poem "Sarah Cynthia Sylvia Stout Would Not Take the Garbage Out."

Parse the following sentences from the book:

1) Sarah Cynthia Sylvia Stout would not take the garbage out!

2) The garbage reached across the state, from New York to the Golden Gate.

Paraphrase the following from "The Worst":
Write your answer on a seperate piece of paper.

3) When singing songs of scariness,
   Of bloodiness and hairyness,
   I feel obligated at this moment to remind you
   Of the most ferocious beast of all:
   Three thousand pounds and nine feet tall—
   The Glurpy Slurpy Skakagrall—
   Who's standing right behind you.

Parse and diagram the following sentences:

4) Shel Silverstein's hilarious poetry is a favorite with children.

5) From his wild imagination, he wrote one poem about a pair of dancing pants.

6) He wrote another one about a man with long, long hair and no clothes.

7) The double-tailed dog can not bite, bark, or growl at you, but he can wag those tails.

8) Silverstein also gives us a recipe for hippopotamus sandwich.

EXERCISE: 5 REINFORCEMENT

Exercise 5: *Stuart Little* by E.B. White

This book is about a small mouse-like person who lives with his family in New York City. Stuart has a great many adventures.

Parse the following sentences from the book:

1) Mr. and Mrs. Little named him Stuart, and Mr. Little made him a tiny bed out of four clothespins and a cigarette box.

2) The home of the Little family was a pleasant place near a park in New York City.

Paraphrase the following from *Stuart Little*:
Write your answer on a seperate piece of paper.

3) When Mrs. Frederick C. Little's second son arrived, everybody noticed that he was not much bigger than a mouse. The truth of the matter was, the baby looked very much like a mouse in every way. He was only about two inches high; and he had a mouse's sharp nose, a mouse's tail, a mouse's whiskers, and the pleasant, shy manner of a mouse.

Reinforcement Exercise: 5

Parse and diagram the following sentences:

4) Stuart Little, his parents, and his brother lived in a house in New York.

5) Stuart was an early riser and he loved the fresh smell of day.

6) Snowball was a cat, and she and Stuart were always in competition with each other.

7) On one terrible day, poor Stuart became lost under the floorboards of the pantry.

8) In his leisure hours, Stuart would sail a toy sailboat on a lake in Central Park.

Exercise: 6 Reinforcement

Exercise 6: *Big Red* by Jim Kjelgaard

This is the story of a young boy who is allowed to take care of a champion show dog, an Irish setter named Red.

Parse the following sentences from the book:

1) The dog had a short leather leash about his neck and was walking, to the left of Robert Fraley, around the ring.

2) Suddenly, Red's thunderous battle roar burst from his throat, and he hurled himself forward.

Paraphrase the following from *Big Red*:

Write your answer on a seperate piece of paper.

3) Forty feet farther on, the tracks of a monster bear emerged from the beeches and joined those of the bull. Danny knelt, and laid his spread hand in the bear's paw mark. The imprinted track was longer and wider than his hand. Old Majesty! Danny rose and skulked on, careful to break no twig, rustle no leaf, and make no other noise that might reveal his coming. A hundred times he had stalked this great bear whose name had become a legend.

REINFORCEMENT **EXERCISE: 6**

Parse and diagram the following sentences:

4) Danny lived with his father in a small cabin on Mr. Haggin's estate and he loved dogs.

5) Big Red was an expensive champion show dog, but he needed a caretaker.

6) Danny could never afford a dog like Red.

7) On a summer morning, Mr. Haggin made Danny the caretaker of Red.

8) Danny and Big Red were inseparable and had many adventures together.

Exercise: 7 Reinforcement

Exercise 7: *To Kill a Mockingbird* by Harper Lee

Young Scout Finch is being raised by her widowed father during the Great Depression. Her father, Atticus, is a lawyer who faces down racism by defending a Black man, something that is not popular among the White people in their town.

Parse the following sentences from the book:

1) It was customary for the men in the family to remain on Simon's homestead, Finch's Landing, and make their living from cotton.

2) I never deliberately learned to read, but somehow I had been wallowing licitly in the daily papers.

Paraphrase the following paragraph:

Write your answer on a seperate piece of paper.

3) Miss Caroline began the day by reading us a story about cats. The cats had long conversations with one another, they wore cunning little clothes and lived in a warm house beneath a kitchen stove. By the time Mrs. Cat called the drugstore for an order of chocolate malted mice the class was wriggling like a bucketful of catawba worms. Miss Caroline seemed unaware that the ragged, denim-shirted and floursack-skirted first grade, most of whom had chopped cotton and fed hogs from the time they were able to walk, were immune to imaginative literature.

Reinforcement Exercise: 7

Parse and diagram the following sentences:

4) Scout, her brother, and her widowed father lived in a small town in the South during the Great Depression.

5) White and Black people were segregated by law at that time, and the races stayed away from each other.

6) Black people could be unfairly charged with crimes, and many White people would not believe the truth.

7) Scout's father was a White lawyer and assigned as public defender for an accused Black man.

8) The people in town did not approve of Atticus's role as defense lawyer for the man.

Exercise: 8   Reinforcement

Exercise 8: *The Hound of the Baskervilles* by Sir Arthur Conan Doyle

This is a mystery about the famous Curse of the Baskervilles. When the head of the house of Baskerville sees the ghastly hound out on the moors, he meets with an untimely death!

Parse the following sentences from the book:

1) Holmes was sitting with his back to me and I had given him no sign of my occupation.

2) The moon was low upon the right, and the jagged pinnacle of a granite tor stood up against the lower curve of its silver disc.

Paraphrase the following paragraph:
Write your answer on a seperate piece of paper.

3) I sprang to my feet, my inert hand grasping my pistol, my mind paralyzed by the dreadful shape which had sprung out upon us from the shadows of the fog. A hound it was, an enormous coal-black hound, but not such a hound as mortal eyes have ever seen. Fire burst from its open mouth, its eyes glowed with a smouldering glare, its muzzle and hackles and dewlap were outlined in flickering flame.

REINFORCEMENT EXERCISE: 8

Parse and diagram the following sentences:

4) Sir Charles Baskerville died, and Sir Henry became the heir to Baskerville Hall.

5) He had received a threatening letter, and his friends were worried about him.

6) Sherlock Holmes and Dr. Watson were helping with the problem.

7) A huge black hound had recently been seen upon the moors in the vicinity.

8) Holmes could not come to Baskerville Hall, but Watson's letters gave him an account of events.

Exercise: 9 Reinforcement

Exercise 9: *The Giver* by Lois Lowry

This novel explores what it could be like to live in a community where everything is truly equal and there is no pain or conflict—at the expense of memories and history and the cultural nuances that make our lives unique. Is this truly a perfect utopia? Jonas is in the position to find out, as the apprentice Receiver of Memories.

Parse the following sentences from the book:

1) He saw only the abandoned bikes here and there on their sides; an upturned wheel on one was still revolving slowly.

2) For a contributing citizen to be released from the community was a final decision, a terrible punishment, an overwhelming statement of failure.

Paraphrase the following paragraph from *The Giver*:

Write your answer on a seperate piece of paper.

3) Though Jonas had only become a Five the year that they acquired Lily and learned her name, he remembered the excitement, the conversations at home, wondering about her: how she would look, who she would be, how she would fit into their established family unit. He remembered climbing the steps to the stage with his parents, his father by his side that year instead of with the Nurturers, since it was the year that he would be given a newchild of his own.

He remembered his mother taking the newchild, his sister, into her arms, while the document was read to the assembled family units. "Newchild Twenty-three," the Namer had read. "Lily."

Reinforcement Exercise: 9

Parse and diagram the following sentences:

4) Jonas's community assigns people specific jobs at the time of their twelfth birthday.

5) The Elders assign Jonas the role of Receiver, and he is surprised and excited.

6) He becomes the apprentice to the current Receiver and receives the memories of the whole community.

7) Some of the memories are shocking and frightening.

8) Their Utopian society grew from many ugly actions, and they are still happening.

Exercise: 10   Reinforcement

Exercise 10: "*Jabberwocky*" by Lewis Carroll

This poem is from the book *Through the Looking Glass*, which tells the story of Alice and her adventures in Wonderland, where things do not always quite make sense.

It's true that these are not the English words you are familiar with; but if you look at them in context and consider the words you do recognize, you should be able to figure out what part of speech these "words" are!

Parse the following sentences from the book:

1) 'Twas brillig, and the slithy toves did gyre and gimble in the wabe.

2) All mimsy were the borogroves, and the mome raths outgrabe.

When trying to parse contractions, you must break the contraction down into the words it was made from.

It would also be helpful to know that "brillig" —according to Mr. Carroll—is approximately tea time!

Paraphrase the following stanza from "Jabberwocky." Make up your own nonsense words, but be sure they FUNCTION grammatically the same as the original words.

Write your answer on a seperate piece of paper.

3) Beware the Jabberwock, my son!
    The jaws that bite and the claws that catch!
    Beware the jubjub bird,
    And shun the frumious bandersnatch!

Reinforcement Exercise: 10

Parse and diagram the following sentences:

1) To some people, this poem does not make any sense.

2) People must use their imaginations in the reading of this poem.

3) In Wonderland, things can be very confusing!

4) Alice bravely faces all the confusion, and she returns finally to her home.

5) Alice's time in Wonderland gives her the adventure of her life!

Exercise: 11 Reinforcement

Exercise 11: *Little Men* by Louisa May Alcott

This book is a sequel to *Little Women* and tells the story of Jo, now a grown woman, and her husband, Professor Bhaer, who run a sort of boarding school for boys who need help.

Parse the following sentences from the book:

1) Through the soft spring rain that fell on sprouting grass and budding trees, Nat saw a large square house before him—a hospitable-looking house, with an old-fashioned porch, wide steps, and shining lights in many windows.

2) Two large rooms on the right were evidently schoolrooms, for desks, maps, blackboards, and books were scattered about.

Paraphrase the following sentences from *Little Men*.
Write your answer on a seperate piece of paper.

3) She was not at all handsome, but she had a merry sort of face, that never seemed to have forgotten certain childish ways and looks, any more than her voice and manner had; and these things, hard to describe but very plain to see and feel, made her a genial, comfortable kind of person, easy to get on with, and generally "jolly," as boys would say.

Parse and diagram the following sentences:

4) Plumfield was the home of Dr. and Mrs. Bhaer, and all sorts of boys lived there.

5) Nat had had a very hard life before his arrival at Plumfield.

6) With Mrs. Bhaer's love and care, Nat found a home at Plumfield.

7) The boys at Plumfield had all sorts of wonderful adventures.

8) Some of the adventures were funny, but some of them were somewhat scary!

Exercise: 12 Reinforcement

Exercise 12: *The Story of Ferdinand* by Munro Leaf

This exercise is from a sweet children's story about a bull named Ferdinand who runs into difficulty when he, a very peaceful bull who loves to sit quietly and smell the flowers, must fight in the big bull ring in Madrid.

Parse the following sentences from the book:

1) It was his favorite tree and he would sit in its shade all day and smell the flowers.

2) The five men saw him and they all shouted with joy.

Paraphrase the following sentences from *The Story of Ferdinand*.
Write your answer on a seperate piece of paper.

3) Once upon a time in Spain there was a little bull and his name was Ferdinand. All the other little bulls he lived with would run and jump and butt their heads together, but not Ferdinand. He liked to sit just quietly and smell the flowers. He had a favorite spot out in the pasture under a cork tree.

Parse and diagram the following sentences:

4) Ferdinand loved his favorite place in the pasture.

5) The men from Madrid picked him, and he was sent to the bullring in Madrid.

6) This was a very great honor for a bull.

7) Ferdinand missed the meadow and his beloved flowers.

8) Ferdinand would always sit and smell the flowers.

Exercise 13: *Black Beauty* by Anna Sewell

This exercise is from a wonderful story told from the point of view of a horse as he goes through the trials and tribulations of life.

Parse the following sentences from the book:

1) I have never forgotten my mother's advice; I knew she was a wise old horse, and our master thought a great deal of her.

2) My ladies have promised that I shall never be sold, and I have nothing to fear; and here my story ends.

Paraphrase the following sentences from *Black Beauty*.
Write your answer on a seperate piece of paper.

3) There was one man, I thought, if he would buy me, I should be happy. He was not a gentleman, nor yet one of the loud, flashy sort that called themselves so. He was rather a small man, but well made, and quick in all his motions. I knew in a moment, by the way he handled me, that he was used to horses; he spoke gently, and his gray eye had a kindly, cheery look in it.

Exercise: 13 Reinforcement

Parse and diagram the following sentences:

4) Black Beauty was born in a meadow on the estate of Squire Gordon.

5) Black Beauty's favorite place was the beautiful meadow at the farm.

6) Squire Gordon could ride on Ginger, and his wife would ride on Black Beauty.

7) The beautiful black thoroughbred was sold to different masters of all sorts.

8) In spite of the difficulties of his life, Black Beauty always did his best.

Exercise 14: "The Sword Excalibur" by Sir Thomas Malory

This story tells of some of the adventures of King Arthur and Merlin the Magician. It is written in an old-fashioned sort of English and is often hard to understand, but the stories about King Arthur are wonderful ones. There are more modern versions of these stories and legends that might be easier for you to read.

Parse the following sentences from the book:

1) Merlin took up King Arthur and rode forth with him upon the knight's horse.

2) So King Arthur and Merlin alighted, tied their horses to two trees, and went into the barge.

Paraphrase the following sentences from "The Sword Excalibur."
Write your answer on a seperate piece of paper.

3) They saw a damsel going upon the lake. "What damsel is that?" said the king.

"That is the Lady of the Lake," said Merlin, "and within that lake is a reach [a small island], and therein is as fair a place as any is on earth, and richly beseen; and this damsel will come to you anon, and then speak fair to her that she will give you that sword."

Therewith came the damsel to King Arthur and saluted him, and he her again.

Exercise: 14 Reinforcement

Parse and diagram the following sentences:

4) King Arthur was the great legendary king of ancient Britain.

5) He may or may not have been real, but we love stories about him.

6) King Arthur's famous sword won him many battles.

7) Merlin was a very wise magician, and he gave Arthur much good advice.

8) King Arthur's castle with the famous Round Table was located in Camelot.

Exercise 15: *The Hobbit, or There and Back Again* by J.R.R. Tolkien

Hobbits are creatures in Tolkien's elaborate fantasy world that love home, comfort, food, and predictability. Bilbo Baggins, the hero of *The Hobbit*, turns his back on all of that and sets off on an epic adventure with a wizard and twelve dwarves.

Parse the following sentences from the book:

1) All that the unsuspecting Bilbo saw that morning was an old man with a staff.

2) "I am looking for someone to share in an adventure that I am arranging, and it's very difficult to find anyone."

Remember, when parsing or diagramming contractions, identify the jobs of the words they are made of.

Paraphrase the following passage from *The Hobbit*:
Write your answer on a seperate piece of paper.

3) "Good morning!" he said at last. "We don't want any adventures here, thank you! You might try over The Hill or across The Water." By this he meant that the conversation was at an end.

"What a lot of things you do use *Good morning* for!" said Gandalf. "Now you mean that you want to get rid of me, and it won't be good till I move off."

"Not at all, not at all, my dear sir! Let me see, I don't think I know your name?"

"Yes, yes, my dear sir—and I do know your name, Mr. Bilbo Baggins. And you do know my name, though you don't remember that I belong to it. I am Gandalf, and Gandalf means me! To think that I should have lived to be good-morninged by Belladonna Took's son, as if I was selling buttons at the door!"

Exercise: 15 Reinforcement

Parse and diagram the following sentences:

4) Bilbo Baggins was a respectable hobbit, and respectable hobbits did not go on adventures.

5) Gandalf wanted Bilbo for his team of adventurers, and Bilbo could not say "no."

6) Thorin Oakenshield was the exiled king of the dwarves, and he sought his hereditary treasure.

7) Bilbo, Gandalf, Thorin, and their companions had many hair-raising adventures in the strange world of Middle-earth.

8) Bilbo wrote his memoirs, and the book was called *There and Back Again.*

Exercise 16: *Anne of Green Gables* by Lucy Maude Montgomery

This is the story of an orphan girl who is adopted by an elderly brother and sister. Anne's sweet nature and vivid imagination change their lives considerably!

Parse the following sentences from the book:

1) When her eyes fell on the odd little figure in the stiff, ugly dress, with the long braids of red hair and the eager luminous eyes, she stopped short in amazement.

Note: This sentence includes a prepositional phrase within a prepositional phrase; be careful!

2) Mrs. Allan took a mouthful of her cake and a most peculiar expression crossed her face.

Paraphrase the following from *Anne of Green Gables*:
Write your answer on a seperate piece of paper.

3) "Anne Shirley, whatever is the matter with you? What have you done? Get right up this minute and tell me. This minute, I say. There now, what is it?"

Anne had slid to the floor in despairing obedience.

"Look at my hair, Marilla," she whispered.

Accordingly, Marilla lifted her candle and looked scrutinizingly at Anne's hair, flowing in heavy masses down her back. It certainly had a very strange appearance.

"Anne Shirley, what have you done to your hair? Why, it's green!"

Exercise: 16 Reinforcement

Parse and diagram the following sentences:

4) Matthew and Marilla needed help on the farm, and they adopted an orphan boy.

5) The "boy" at the train station was really a little girl with red hair.

6) Young Anne Shirley completely changed the lives of Matthew and Marilla.

7) Anne's vivid imagination and impetuous nature led her to many adventures.

8) Anne stayed with the Cuthberts, and then she had a wonderful life.

Exercise 17: *When We Were Very Young* by A. A. Milne

This exercise is from a book of children's poems. Mr. Milne wrote many stories about Christopher Robin and his favorite bear (of the Teddy variety) named Winnie the Pooh.

Parse the following sentences from the book:

1) They're changing guard at Buckingham Palace, and Christopher Robin went down with Alice.

2) Ernest was an elephant, a great big fellow; Leonard was a lion with a six-foot tail; George was a goat, and his head was yellow; and James was a very small snail.

Paraphrase the following from *When We Were Very Young*:

Write your answer on a seperate piece of paper.

3) Whenever I walk in a London Street,
I'm ever so careful to watch my feet;
    And I keep in the squares,
    And the masses of bears,
Who wait at the corners all ready to eat
The sillies who tread on the lines of the street, Go
    back to their lairs,
    And I say to them, "Bears,
Just look how I'm walking in all of the squares!"

Exercise: 17 Reinforcement

Parse and diagram the following sentences:

1) For decades, A. A. Milne wrote many poems and stories for children.

2) "Daffodowndilly" is a poem about a daffodil and it is a favorite.

3) The central character in these poems has a great friend by the name of Pooh.

4) Christopher Robin has many toys, and his very favorite one is Winnie the Pooh.

5) A. A. Milne has been popular with children and their parents for a very long time.

Exercise 18: *Mary Poppins* by P. L. Travers

This collection of short stories tells of the adventures of Jane and Michael Banks, two little English children, and their extraordinary and magical nanny.

Parse the following sentences from the book:

1) Upstairs in the nursery, Jane and Michael watched at the window and wondered who would come.

2) With her large bag in her hands she slid gracefully UP the banisters and arrived at the landing at the same time as Mrs. Banks.

Paraphrase the following from *Mary Poppins*:

Write your answer on a seperate piece of paper.

3) "Well," said Mary Poppins, "it's all very silly and undignified, but, since you're all up there and don't seem able to get down, I suppose I'd better come up, too."

With that, to the surprise of Jane and Michael, she put her hands down at her sides and without a laugh, without even the faintest glimmer of a smile, she shot up through the air and sat down beside Jane.

"How many times, I should like to know," she said snappily, "have I told you to take off your coat when you come into a hot room?" And she unbuttoned Jane's coat and laid it neatly on the air beside the hat.

Exercise: 18 Reinforcement

Parse and diagram the following sentences:

4) Jane and Michael were two children of a family on Cherry Tree Lane in London.

5) The Bankses needed a new nanny for their children, and they advertised for one.

6) They put an advertisement in the paper and hoped for a well-qualified person.

7) Nobody but Mary Poppins came to their house in answer to the advertisement.

8) She had wonderful magical powers, and incredible things always happened on an outing with her.

Level 3
Reinforcement Answer Key

Exercise 1: *The Wind in the Willows* by Kenneth Grahame

This exercise is taken from a book which tells of the adventures of Badger, Rat, Mole, and Mr. Toad, who all live by the riverbank.

Parse the following sentences from the book:

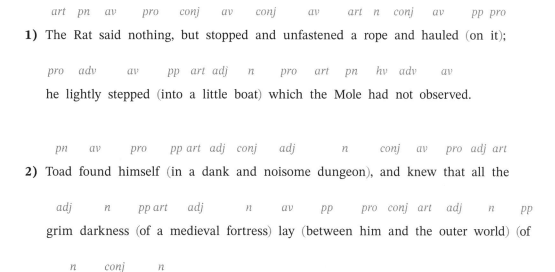

1) The Rat said nothing, but stopped and unfastened a rope and hauled (on it);
   art pn av pro conj av conj av art n conj av pp pro

   he lightly stepped (into a little boat) which the Mole had not observed.
   pro adv av pp art adj n pro art pn hv adv av

2) Toad found himself (in a dank and noisome dungeon), and knew that all the
   pn av pro pp art adj conj adj n conj av pro adj art

   grim darkness (of a medieval fortress) lay (between him and the outer world) (of
   adj n pp art adj n av pp pro conj art adj n pp

   sunshine and highroads).
   n conj n

Paraphrase the following from *The Wind in the Willows*:
Write your answer on a separate piece of paper.

3) The following evening the Mole, who had risen late and taken things very easy all day, was sitting on the bank fishing, when the Rat, who had been looking up his friends and gossiping, came strolling along to find him. "Heard the news?" he said. "There's nothing else being talked about, all along the river bank. Toad went up to Town by an early train this morning. And he has ordered a large and very expensive motorcar."

Answers on these paraphrases will vary. Evaluate them based on how many key words were actually changed and how well the paraphrase covers the original meaning.

Exercise: 1 Reinforcement Answer Key

Parse and diagram the following sentences:

```
        ──pn──    lv  art  adv     adj        n    conj  pro  hv   adv    av   adj    n
4)  Mr. Toad was a very enthusiastic creature, and he was always getting bright ideas.


         adj       n     adv      av      pro   pp     n
5)  His enthusiasms often pitchforked him (into trouble).


     pn    av  art  adj   adj      n    conj pro   av   pro    adv
6)  Toad saw a shiny new motorcar, and he wanted one immediately.


       n     lv  adv adj  adj      n     conj pro   av    pp  adj   n    pp    n
7)  Driving was not his best accomplishment, and he crashed (into all sorts) (of things).


      adj    adj    n    pp  art     n     av   pn   pp  adj    n    pp   art
8)  Toad's animal friends (on the riverbank) kept Toad (in his house) (until the

     n   pp  adj   n
    end) (of this fad).
```

Exercise 1: *The Wind in the Willows* by Kenneth Grahame

4)
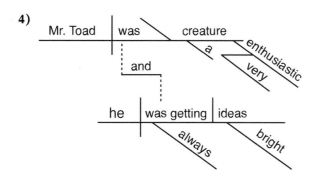

5)
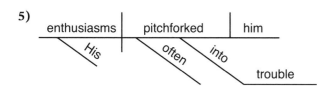

6)
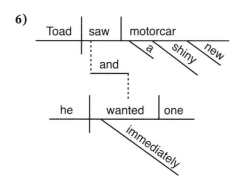

7)
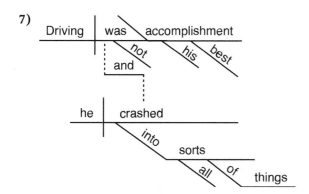

8)
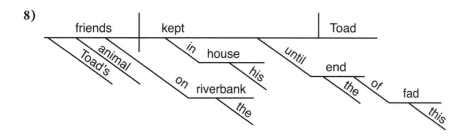

Exercise: 2 — Reinforcement Answer Key

Exercise 2: *National Velvet* by Enid Bagnold

This is the story of a horse-mad young girl who is given a pony which she trains for the Grand National, the greatest horse race in England.

Parse the following sentences from the book:

1)
   pn   av   art   n   pp   n   conj art   n   av   adj   n   adv   pp art

Velvet produced a piece (of sugar) and the pony bent her head round (with a

   n   pp   n

look) (of insolence.)

2)
   pn art   adj   adj   n   pro   pro   av   adv   av   art   n   pp   pn   conj —pro—

(In the one local paper) which they took there was a lot (about Velvet), but no one

   av   —v—   adv pp adj art   adj   n

thought to send out (for all the other papers).

Paraphrase the following from *National Velvet*:

Write your answer on a seperate piece of paper.

3) "Stop! Stand! He's never going over that!"

The ground had dropped away so sharply at the far corner that the original builder of the cobbled wall, to keep his coping straight, had heightened the wall itself. It was five feet two at the end of the field, with a fine downhill take-off. The horse sailed over like a dappled flying boat. It was a double spring. As he was high in the air he saw also to his hind feet and drew them up sharply.

"...AND to spare," said Mi quietly, nodding his head. "A horse like that'd win the National."

Answers on these paraphrases will vary. Evaluate them based on how many key words were actually changed and how well the paraphrase covers the original meaning.

Reinforcement Answer Key **Exercise: 2**

Parse and diagram the following sentences:

        pn   *av*   *n*   *pp* *adj* *adj*   *n*   *conj*   *adv*   *av*   *pro* *pp* *adj*   *n*

4) Velvet loved horses (with all her heart) and desperately wanted one (of her own).

     pp   *art*   *n*   *pp*   *art*   *adj*   *n*   *pn*   *av* *art*   *n*   *pp* *art*   *n*

5) (On the day) (of the village fair), Velvet won a horse (in a raffle).

     adj   *n*   *hv*   *av*   *pp* *adj*   *n*   *conj* *av*   *adv*   *pp*   *art*   *n*

6) This horse would jump (over tall fences) and run madly (through the town).

     adj   *adj*   *n*   *lv*   *adj*   *n* *pp* *art* ———*pn*———

7) Velvet's secret dream was first prize (in the Grand National).

     adj   *n*   *pp*   *pn* *conj* *adj*   *adj*   *n*   *lv* *pro* *pp* *art*   *adj*

8) The story (of Velvet and her astonishing horse) is one (of the best-loved

    n   *pp* *adj* *n*

stories) (of all time).

Exercise 2: *National Velvet* by Enid Bagnold

4)
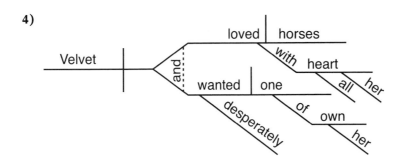

5)
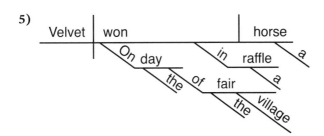

6)
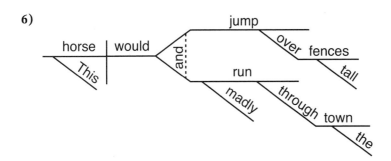

7)
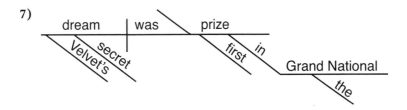

8)
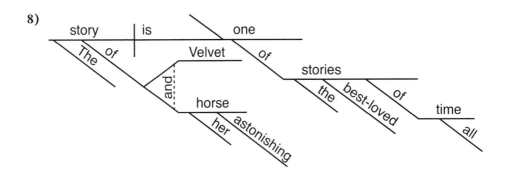

Exercise 3: *Holes* by Louis Sachar

This book is about a boy named Stanley who is falsely accused of a crime and sent to a detention camp. There are some strange things going on at Camp Green Lake!

Parse the following sentences from the book:

1) Everyone (in his family) had always liked the fact that "Stanley Yelnats" was spelled the
   pro pp adj n   hv   adv   av   art n   pro ———pn——— hv   av art

   same frontward and backward.
   n   adv   conj adv

2) Stanley and his parents didn't believe (in curses), (of course), but whenever anything
   pn conj adj   n   hv/adv   av   pp   n   pp   n   conj adv   pro

   went wrong, it felt good to be able to blame someone.
   lv   adj pro lv adj —v— adj —v—   pro

When parsing or diagramming a contraction, you must break it into its separate words and identify each part. The word *didn't* is a combination of *did* and *not*. The apostrophe represents a missing letter, and the two words have been combined into one. So in this example, *didn't* would be parsed as *hv/adv*, because *did* is doing the job of a helping verb, while *n(o)t* is an adverb.

Paraphrase the following from *Holes*:
Write your answer on a seperate piece of paper.

3) There is no lake at Camp Green Lake. There once was a very large lake here, the largest lake in Texas. That was over a hundred years ago. Now it is just a dry, flat wasteland.

   There used to be a town of Green Lake as well. The town shriveled and dried up along with the lake, and the people who lived there.

   During the summer the daytime temperature hovers around ninety-five degrees in the shade—if you can find any shade. There's not much shade in a big dry lake.

Answers on these paraphrases will vary. Evaluate them based on how many key words were actually changed and how well the paraphrase covers the original meaning.

Exercise: 3 Reinforcement Answer Key

Parse and diagram the following sentences:

4) ─── pn ───   lv   art   n   pp   art   adj   n   pp   pro   pp   adj   n
   Stanley Yelnats is a boy (from a poor family) (with nothing) (but bad luck).

5) pro   lv   adv   adj   pp   art   n   conj   av   pp ─── pn ─── pp   art   adj
   He is falsely accused (of a crime) and sent (to Camp Green Lake) (in the arid

   adj   n
   Texas desert).

6) art   n   pp   art   n   hv   av   art   adj   n   adv   conj   pro   hv   lv   adv   adj
   The boys (at the camp) must dig a deep hole daily, or they will be harshly punished.

7) art   pn   av   pro   pp   art   n   pp   adj   n   av   adv   pn
   The Warden rewards them (for the discovery) (of "interesting" things), and soon Stanley

   lv   adj
   becomes suspicious.

8) pro   hv   hv   av   pp   art   adj   n   pp ─── pn ───
   Anything could be hidden in the dried-up bed of (Green Lake)!

Exercise 3: *Holes* by Louis Sachar

4)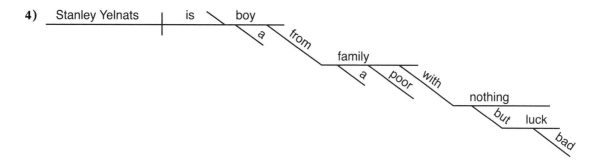

5)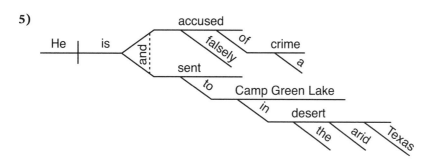

6)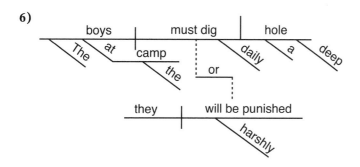

7)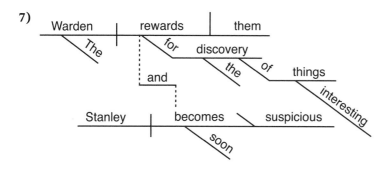

8)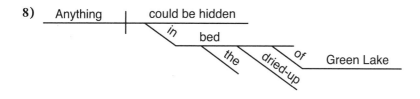

Exercise: 4 Reinforcement Answer Key

Exercise 4: *Where the Sidewalk Ends* by Shel Silverstein

This exercise is from a book of poems for children and young people. These two sentences are from the poem "Sarah Cynthia Sylvia Stout Would Not Take the Garbage Out."

Parse the following sentences from the book:

————————pn———————— hv   adv   av   art   n   adv
1) Sarah Cynthia Sylvia Stout would not take the garbage out!

art   n   av   pp   art   n   pp ——pn—— pp art ——pn——
2) The garbage reached (across the state), (from New York) (to the Golden Gate).

Paraphrase the following from "The Worst":
Write your answer on a seperate piece of paper.

3) When singing songs of scariness,
   Of bloodiness and hairyness,
   I feel obligated at this moment to remind you
   Of the most ferocious beast of all:
   Three thousand pounds and nine feet tall—
   The Glurpy Slurpy Skakagrall—
   Who's standing right behind you.

Answers on these paraphrases will vary. Evaluate them based on how many key words were actually changed and how well the paraphrase covers the original meaning.

Parse and diagram the following sentences:

————adj————   adj   n   lv art   n   pp   n
4) Shel Silverstein's hilarious poetry is a favorite (with children).

pp   adj adj   n   pro   av adj   n   pp art   n   pp adj   n
5) (From his wild imagination), he wrote one poem (about a pair) (of dancing pants).

pro   av   adj   pro   pp art   n   pp   adj   adj   n   conj adj   n
6) He wrote another one (about a man) (with long, long hair and no clothes.)

art   adj   n   hv adv av   av conj av   pp pro conj pro hv   av   adj   n
7) The double-tailed dog can not bite, bark, or growl (at you), but he can wag those tails.

pn   adv av pro art   n   pp   adj   n
8) Silverstein also gives us a recipe (for hippopotamus sandwich).

Exercise 4: *Where the Sidewalk Ends* by Shel Silverstein

4)
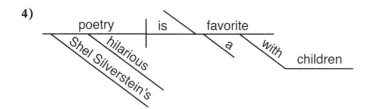

5)
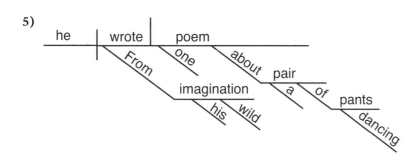

6)
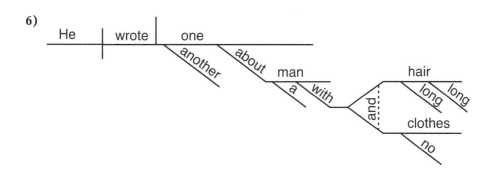

7)
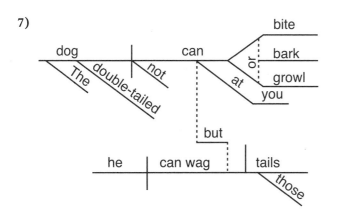

8)
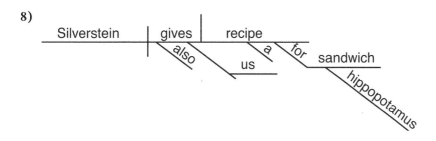

EXERCISE: 5   REINFORCEMENT ANSWER KEY

Exercise 5: *Stuart Little* by E.B. White

This book is about a small mouse-like person who lives with his family in New York City. Stuart has a great many adventures.

Parse the following sentences from the book:

```
      pn  conj ——pn——   av   pro   pn   conj ——pn——   av  pro art adj   n   ——pp——  adj
1) Mr. and Mrs. Little named him Stuart, and Mr. Little made him a tiny bed (out of four

         n     conj art  adj    n
   clothespins and a cigarette box).


      art   n    pp art  adj    n    lv art  adj    n   pp art   n   pp  ———pn———
2) The home (of the Little family) was a pleasant place (near a park) (in New York City).
```

Paraphrase the following from *Stuart Little*:
Write your answer on a seperate piece of paper.

3) When Mrs. Frederick C. Little's second son arrived, everybody noticed that he was not much bigger than a mouse. The truth of the matter was, the baby looked very much like a mouse in every way. He was only about two inches high; and he had a mouse's sharp nose, a mouse's tail, a mouse's whiskers, and the pleasant, shy manner of a mouse.

Answers on these paraphrases will vary. Evaluate them based on how many key words were actually changed and how well the paraphrase covers the original meaning.

Reinforcement Answer Key   **Exercise: 5**

Parse and diagram the following sentences:

    ———pn———   adj   n   conj   adj   n   av   pp   art   n   pp ———pn———

4) Stuart Little, his parents, and his brother lived (in a house) (in New York).

     pn   lv   art   adj   n   conj   pro   av   art   adj   n   pp   n

5) Stuart was an early riser and he loved the fresh smell (of day).

     pn   lv   art   n   conj   pro   conj   pn   av   adv   pp   n   pp   adj   pro

6) Snowball was a cat, and she and Stuart were always (in competition) (with each other.)

     pp   adj   adj   n   adj   pn   lv   adj   pp   art   n   pp   art   n

7) (On one terrible day), poor Stuart became lost (under the floorboards) (of the pantry).

     pp   adj   adj   n   pn   hv   av   art   adj   n   pp   art   n   pp ———pn———

8) (In his leisure hours), Stuart would sail a toy sailboat (on a lake) (in Central Park).

Exercise 5: *Stuart Little* by E.B. White

4)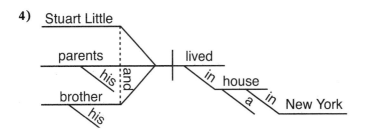

5)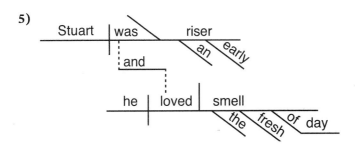

6)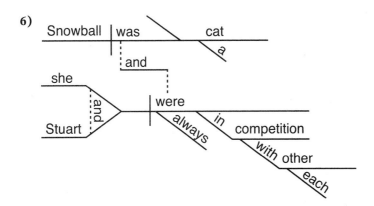

7)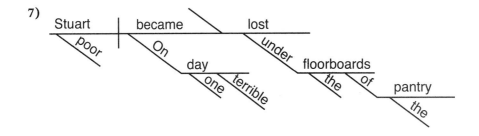

8)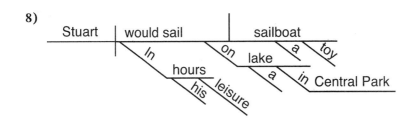

Exercise 6: *Big Red* by Jim Kjelgaard

This is the story of a young boy who is allowed to take care of a champion show dog, an Irish setter named Red.

Parse the following sentences from the book:

1)
```
    art   n   av  art  adj    adj    n    pp   adj   n   conj  hv    av   pp art   n
```
The dog had a short leather leash (about his neck) and was walking, (to the left)

```
 pp ——pn—— pp   art   n
```
(of Robert Fraley), (around the ring).

2)
```
   adv    adj    adj    adj    n   av   pp  adj   n   conj pro   av
```
Suddenly, Red's thunderous battle roar burst (from his throat), and he hurled

```
 pro    adv
```
himself forward.

Paraphrase the following from *Big Red*:
Write your answer on a seperate piece of paper.

3) Forty feet farther on, the tracks of a monster bear emerged from the beeches and joined those of the bull. Danny knelt, and laid his spread hand in the bear's paw mark. The imprinted track was longer and wider than his hand. Old Majesty! Danny rose and skulked on, careful to break no twig, rustle no leaf, and make no other noise that might reveal his coming. A hundred times he had stalked this great bear whose name had become a legend.

Answers on these paraphrases will vary. Evaluate them based on how many key words were actually changed and how well the paraphrase covers the original meaning.

Exercise: 6   Reinforcement Answer Key

Parse and diagram the following sentences:

      pn   av   pp adj   n   pp art adj   n   pp ——adj——   n conj pro

4) Danny lived (with his father) (in a small cabin) (on Mr. Haggin's estate) and he

  av   n

loved dogs.

   ——pn—— lv   art   adj   adj   adj   n conj pro av art   n

5) Big Red was an expensive champion show dog, but he needed a caretaker.

   pn   hv   adv   av art n   pp   pn

6) Danny could never afford a dog (like Red).

  pp art   adj   n   ——pn—— av   pn art   n   pp pn

7) (On a summer morning), Mr. Haggin made Danny the caretaker (of Red).

  pn conj ——pn—— lv   adj   conj av   adj   n   adv

8) Danny and Big Red were inseparable and had many adventures together.

Exercise 6: *Big Red* by Jim Kjelgaard

4)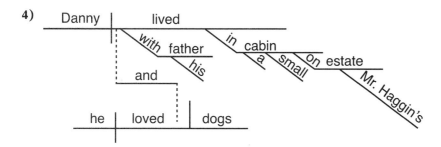

5)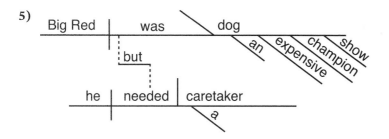

6)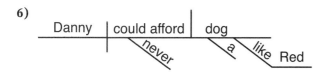

7)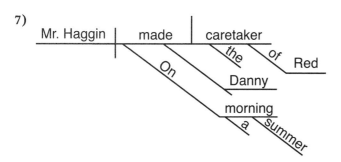

8)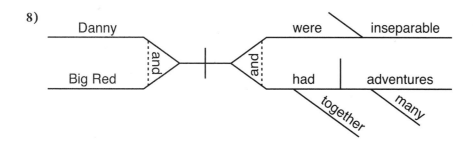

Exercise: 7 Reinforcement Answer Key

Exercise 7: *To Kill a Mockingbird* by Harper Lee

Young Scout Finch is being raised by her widowed father during the Great Depression. Her father, Atticus, is a lawyer who faces down racism by defending a Black man, something that is not popular among the White people in their town.

Parse the following sentences from the book:

    pro lv   adj   pp art   n   pp art   n   ——v—— pp   adj   n

1) It was customary (for the men) (in the family) to remain (on Simon's homestead),

      ——pn—— conj av   adj   n   pp   n

Finch's Landing, and make their living (from cotton).

  pn adv   adv   av ——v—— conj   adv   pro hv   hv   av   adv

2) I never deliberately learned to read, but somehow I had been wallowing licitly

    pp art adj   n

(in the daily papers).

Paraphrase the following paragraph:

Write your answer on a seperate piece of paper.

3) Miss Caroline began the day by reading us a story about cats. The cats had long conversations with one another, they wore cunning little clothes and lived in a warm house beneath a kitchen stove. By the time Mrs. Cat called the drugstore for an order of chocolate malted mice the class was wriggling like a bucketful of catawba worms. Miss Caroline seemed unaware that the ragged, denim-shirted and floursack-skirted first grade, most of whom had chopped cotton and fed hogs from the time they were able to walk, were immune to imaginative literature.

Answers on these paraphrases will vary. Evaluate them based on how many key words were actually changed and how well the paraphrase covers the original meaning.

REINFORCEMENT ANSWER KEY — EXERCISE: 7

Parse and diagram the following sentences:

        pn   *adj*   *n*   *conj* *adj*   *adj*   *n*   *av*   *pp* *art* *adj*   *n*   *pp* *art* *pn*

4) Scout, her brother, and her widowed father lived (in a small town) (in the South)

     pp   *art* ——————*pn*——————

(during the Great Depression).

     adj *conj* *adj*   *n*   *lv*   *adj*   *pp* *n*   *pp* *adj*   *n*   *conj* *art*   *n*   *av*

5) White and Black people were segregated (by law) (at that time), and the races stayed

   adv   *pp*   *adj*   *n*

away (from each other).

    adj   *n*   *hv*   *hv*   *adv*   *av*   *pp*   *n*   *conj* *adj* *adj*   *n*   *hv*   *adv*

6) Black people could be unfairly charged (with crimes,) and many White people would not

    av   *art* *n*

believe the truth.

   adj   *n*   *lv* *adv* *adj*   *n*   *conj*   *av*   *pp* *adj*   *n*   *pp* *art* *adj*

7) Scout's father was a White lawyer and assigned (as public defender) (for an accused

   adj   *n*

Black man).

   art   *n*   *pp*   *n*   *hv* *adv*   *av*   *pp*   *adj*   *n*   *pp* *adj*   *n*   *pp*

8) The people (in town) did not approve (of Atticus's role) (as defense lawyer) (for

  adj *n*

the man).

Exercise 7: To Kill a Mockingbird by Harper Lee

4)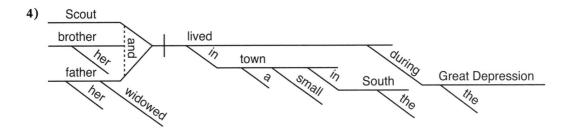

5)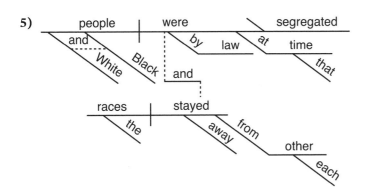

6)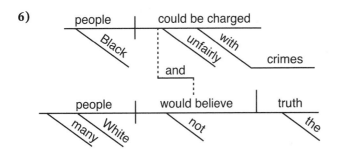

7)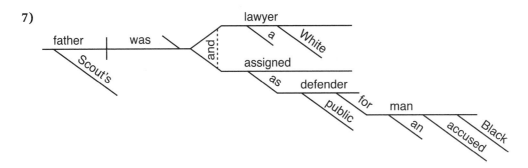

8)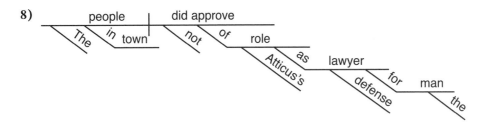

Exercise 8: *The Hound of the Baskervilles* by Sir Arthur Conan Doyle

This is a mystery about the famous Curse of the Baskervilles. When the head of the house of Baskerville sees the ghastly hound out on the moors, he meets with an untimely death!

Parse the following sentences from the book:

1) *pn* Holmes *hv* was *av* sitting (*pp* with *adj* his *n* back) (*pp* to *pro* me) *conj* and *pro* I *hv* had *av* given *pro* him *adj* no *n* sign (*pp* of *adj* my *n* occupation).

2) *art* The *n* moon *lv* was *adj* low (*pp* upon *art* the *n* right), *conj* and *art* the *adj* jagged *n* pinnacle (*pp* of *art* a *adj* granite *n* tor) *av* stood *adv* up (*pp* against *art* the *adj* lower *n* curve) (*pp* of *adj* its *adj* silver *n* disc).

Paraphrase the following paragraph:
Write your answer on a seperate piece of paper.

3) I sprang to my feet, my inert hand grasping my pistol, my mind paralyzed by the dreadful shape which had sprung out upon us from the shadows of the fog. A hound it was, an enormous coal-black hound, but not such a hound as mortal eyes have ever seen. Fire burst from its open mouth, its eyes glowed with a smouldering glare, its muzzle and hackles and dewlap were outlined in flickering flame.

Answers on these paraphrases will vary. Evaluate them based on how many key words were actually changed and how well the paraphrase covers the original meaning.

Exercise: 8   Reinforcement Answer Key

Parse and diagram the following sentences:

———pn——— av   conj ——pn—— lv   art   n   pp ——pn——
4) Sir Charles Baskerville died, and Sir Henry became the heir (to Baskerville Hall).

pro   hv   av   art   adj   n   conj adj   n   lv   adj   pp   pro
5) He had received a threatening letter, and his friends were worried (about him).

——pn—— conj ——pn—— hv   av   pp   art   n
6) Sherlock Holmes and Dr. Watson were helping (with the problem).

art adj adj   n   hv   adv   hv   av   pp art   n   pp art   n
7) A huge black hound had recently been seen (upon the moors) (in the vicinity).

pn   hv   adv   av   pp ——pn—— conj adj   n   av   pro
8) Holmes could not come (to Baskerville Hall), but Watson's letters gave him

art   n   pp   n
an account (of events).

Exercise 8:
The Hound of the Baskervilles by Sir Arthur Conan Doyle

4)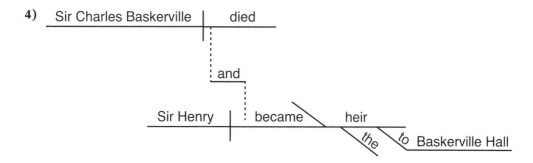

5)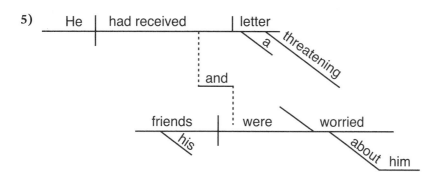

6)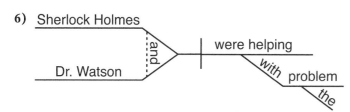

7)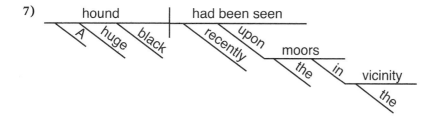

8)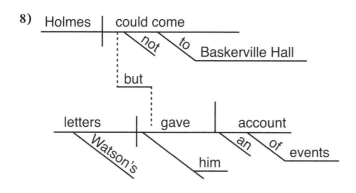

EXERCISE: 9 REINFORCEMENT ANSWER KEY

Exercise 9: *The Giver* by Lois Lowry

This novel explores what it could be like to live in a community where everything is truly equal and there is no pain or conflict—at the expense of memories and history and the cultural nuances that make our lives unique. Is this truly a perfect utopia? Jonas is in the position to find out, as the apprentice Receiver of Memories.

Parse the following sentences from the book:

1)   pn av adv art adj   n   adv conj adv pp adj   n   art   adj   n
    He saw only the abandoned bikes here and there (on their sides); an upturned wheel

    pp pro   hv adv   av   adv
    (on one) was still revolving slowly.

2)   pp art   adj   n   —v—   av   pp art   n   lv art adj   n   art
    (For a contributing citizen) to be released (from the community) was a final decision, a

    adj   n   art   adj   n   pp   n
    terrible punishment, an overwhelming statement (of failure).

Paraphrase the following paragraph from *The Giver*:

Write your answer on a seperate piece of paper.

3) Though Jonas had only become a Five the year that they acquired Lily and learned her name, he remembered the excitement, the conversations at home, wondering about her: how she would look, who she would be, how she would fit into their established family unit. He remembered climbing the steps to the stage with his parents, his father by his side that year instead of with the Nurturers, since it was the year that he would be given a newchild of his own.

He remembered his mother taking the newchild, his sister, into her arms, while the document was read to the assembled family units. "Newchild Twenty-three," the Namer had read. "Lily."

Answers on these paraphrases will vary. Evaluate them based on how many key words were actually changed and how well the paraphrase covers the original meaning.

Parse and diagram the following sentences:

       adj   *n*   *v*   *n*   *adj*   *adv* *pp* *art*   *n*   *pp* *adj*   *adj*   *n*

4) Jonas's community assigns people specific jobs (at the time) (of their twelfth birthday).

       art   *pn*   *av*   *pn*   *art*   *n*   *pp*   *pn*   *av* *pro* *lv*   *adj*   *conj* *adj*

5) The Elders assign Jonas the role (of Receiver,) and he is surprised and excited.

      pro   *lv*   *art*   *n*   *pp* *art*   *adj*   *pn*   *conj*   *av*   *art*   *n*   *pp* *art*

6) He becomes the apprentice (to the current Receiver) and receives the memories (of the

      adj   *n*

whole community).

      pro *pp* *art*   *n*   *lv*   *adj*   *conj*   *adj*

7) Some (of the memories) are shocking and frightening.

      adj   *adj*   *n*   *av*   *pp* *adj* *adj*   *n*   *conj* *pro* *lv* *adv*   *adj*

8) Their Utopian society grew (from many ugly actions), and they are still happening.

Exercise 9: *The Giver* by Lois Lowry

4)
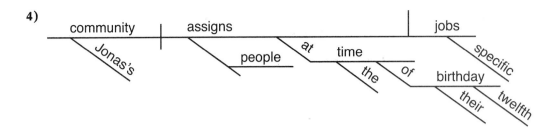

5)
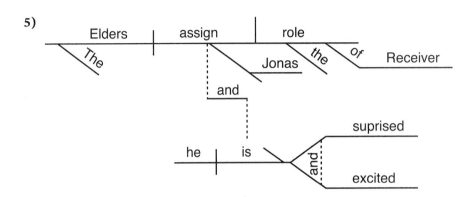

6)
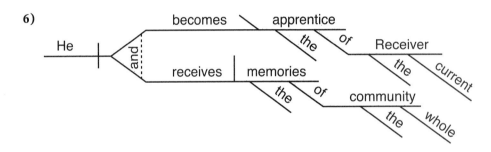

7)
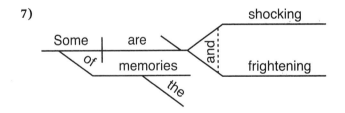

8)
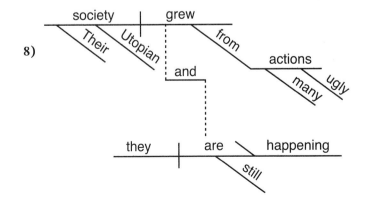

Exercise 10: *"Jabberwocky"* by Lewis Carroll

This poem is from the book *Through the Looking Glass*, which tells the story of Alice and her adventures in Wonderland, where things do not always quite make sense.

It's true that these are not the English words you are familiar with; but if you look at them in context and consider the words you do recognize, you should be able to figure out what part of speech these "words" are!

Parse the following sentences from the book:

    pro/lv   n   conj art adj   n   hv   av conj   av   pp   art   n

1) 'Twas brillig, and the slithy toves did gyre and gimble (in the wabe).

    adv   adj   lv   art   n   conj art   adj   n   av

2) All mimsy were the borogroves, and the mome raths outgrabe.

When trying to parse contractions, you must break the contraction down into the words it was made from.

It would also be helpful to know that "brillig" —according to Mr. Carroll—is approximately tea time!

Paraphrase the following stanza from "Jabberwocky." Make up your own nonsense words, but be sure they FUNCTION grammatically the same as the original words.

Write your answer on a seperate piece of paper.

3) Beware the Jabberwock, my son!
    The jaws that bite and the claws that catch!
    Beware the jubjub bird,
    And shun the frumious bandersnatch!

Answers on these paraphrases will vary. Evaluate them based on how many key words were actually changed and how well the paraphrase covers the original meaning.

Exercise: 10   Reinforcement Answer Key

Parse and diagram the following sentences:

     pp   *adj*   *n*   *adj*   *n*   *hv* *adv* *av* *adj*   *n*

1) (To some people,) this poem does not make any sense.

    n   *hv* *av* *adj*   *n*   *pp* *art*   *n*   *pp* *adj*   *n*

2) People must use their imaginations (in the reading) (of this poem).

    pp   *pn*   *n*   *hv* *lv* *adv*   *adj*

3) (In Wonderland,) things can be very confusing!

    pn   *adv*   *av* *adj* *art*   *n*   *conj* *pro*   *av*   *adv* *pp* *adj*   *n*

4) Alice bravely faces all the confusion, and she returns finally (to her home).

   adj   *n* *pp*   *pn*   *av* *pro* *art*   *n*   *pp* *adj* *n*

5) Alice's time (in Wonderland) gives her the adventure (of her life)!

Exercise 10: "Jabberwocky" Lewis Carroll

4)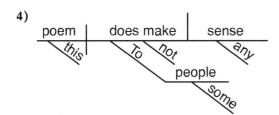

5)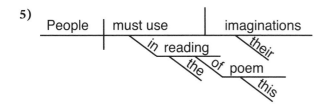

6)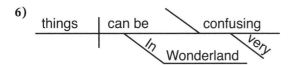

7)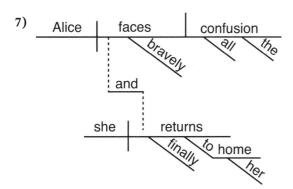

8)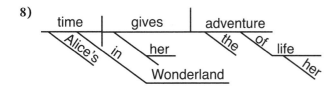

Exercise 11: *Little Men* by Louisa May Alcott

This book is a sequel to *Little Women* and tells the story of Jo, now a grown woman, and her husband, Professor Bhaer, who run a sort of boarding school for boys who need help.

Parse the following sentences from the book:

1)
```
   pp   art adj  adj    n   pro av  pp    adj       n    conj  adj    n
```
(Through the soft spring rain) that fell (on sprouting grass and budding trees),

```
    pn  av art  adj   adj     n    pp  pro art       adj          n    pp  art
```
Nat saw a large square house (before him)—a hospitable-looking house, (with an

```
      adj         n    adj    n   conj  adj      n    pp   adj     n
```
old-fashioned porch, wide steps, and shining lights) (in many windows).

2)
```
   adj  adj    n   pp art    n    lv   adv         n     conj   n     n
```
Two large rooms (on the right) were evidently schoolrooms, for desks, maps,

```
     n    conj  n    hv    av    adv
```
blackboards, and books were scattered about.

Paraphrase the following sentences from *Little Men*.
Write your answer on a seperate piece of paper.

3) She was not at all handsome, but she had a merry sort of face, that never seemed to have forgotten certain childish ways and looks, any more than her voice and manner had; and these things, hard to describe but very plain to see and feel, made her a genial, comfortable kind of person, easy to get on with, and generally "jolly," as boys would say.

Answers on these paraphrases will vary. Evaluate them based on how many key words were actually changed and how well the paraphrase covers the original meaning.

Reinforcement Answer Key — Exercise: 11

Parse and diagram the following sentences:

4) <u>pn</u>   <u>lv</u> <u>art</u> <u>n</u>   <u>pp</u> <u>pn</u> <u>conj</u> ——<u>pn</u>—— <u>conj</u> <u>adj</u> <u>n</u>   <u>pp</u> <u>n</u>
Plumfield was the home (of Dr. and Mrs. Bhaer,) and all sorts (of boys)
<u>av</u>   <u>adv</u>
lived there.

5) <u>pn</u> <u>hv</u> <u>av</u> <u>art</u> <u>adv</u> <u>adj</u> <u>n</u>   <u>pp</u>   <u>adj</u> <u>n</u>   <u>pp</u>   <u>pn</u>
Nat had had a very hard life (before his arrival) (at Plumfield).

6) <u>pp</u>   ——<u>adj</u>—— <u>n</u> <u>conj</u> <u>n</u>   <u>pn</u> <u>av</u> <u>art</u> <u>n</u>   <u>pp</u>   <u>pn</u>
(With Mrs. Bhaer's love and care), Nat found a home (at Plumfield).

7) <u>art</u> <u>n</u>   <u>pp</u>   <u>pn</u>   <u>av</u> <u>adj</u> <u>n</u>   <u>pp</u>   <u>adj</u>   <u>n</u>
The boys (at Plumfield) had all sorts (of wonderful adventures).

8) <u>pro</u> <u>pp</u> <u>art</u>   <u>n</u>   <u>lv</u> <u>adj</u> <u>conj</u> <u>pro</u> <u>pp</u> <u>pro</u> <u>lv</u>   <u>adv</u>   <u>adj</u>
Some (of the adventures) were funny, but some (of them) were somewhat scary!

Exercise 11: Little Men by Louisa May Alcott

4)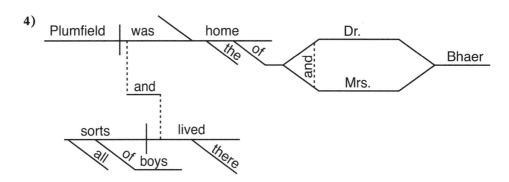

5)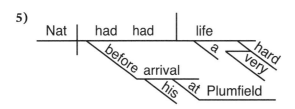

6)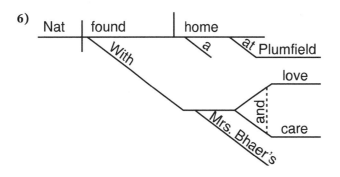

7)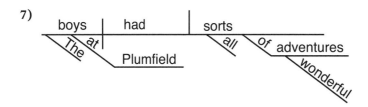

8)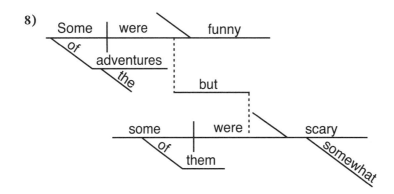

Exercise 12: *The Story of Ferdinand* by Munro Leaf

This exercise is from a sweet children's story about a bull named Ferdinand who runs into difficulty when he, a very peaceful bull who loves to sit quietly and smell the flowers, must fight in the big bull ring in Madrid.

Parse the following sentences from the book:

1) pro lv adj adj n conj pro hv av pp adj n adj n conj av
   It was his favorite tree and he would sit (in its shade) all day and smell

   art n
   the flowers.

2) art adj n av pro conj pro pro av pp n
   The five men saw him and they all shouted (with joy).

Paraphrase the following sentences from *The Story of Ferdinand*.
Write your answer on a seperate piece of paper.

3) Once upon a time in Spain there was a little bull and his name was Ferdinand. All the other little bulls he lived with would run and jump and butt their heads together, but not Ferdinand. He liked to sit just quietly and smell the flowers. He had a favorite spot out in the pasture under a cork tree.

Answers on these paraphrases will vary. Evaluate them based on how many key words were actually changed and how well the paraphrase covers the original meaning.

Parse and diagram the following sentences:

4) pn av adj adj n pp art n
   Ferdinand loved his favorite place (in the pasture).

5) art n pp pn av pro conj pro hv av pp art n pp pn
   The men (from Madrid) picked him, and he was sent (to the bullring) (in Madrid).

6) pro lv art adv adj n pp art n
   This was a very great honor (for a bull).

7) pn av art n conj adj adj n
   Ferdinand missed the meadow and his beloved flowers.

8) pn hv adv av conj av art n
   Ferdinand would always sit and smell the flowers.

Exercise 12: The Story of Ferdinand by Munro Leaf

4)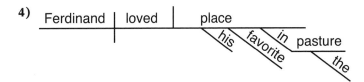

5)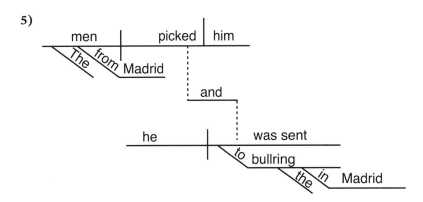

6)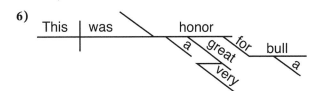

7)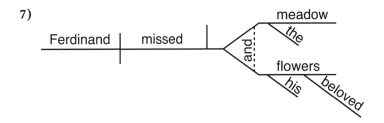

8)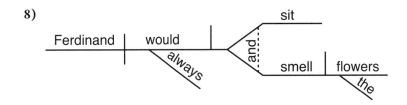

Exercise 13: *Black Beauty* by Anna Sewell

This exercise is from a wonderful story told from the point of view of a horse as he goes through the trials and tribulations of life.

Parse the following sentences from the book:

1) *pro* I *lv* have *adv* never *av* forgotten *adv* my *adj* mother's *n* advice; *pro* I *av* knew *pro* she *lv* was *art* a *adj* wise *adj* old *n* horse, *conj* and *adj* our *n* master *av* thought *art* a *adj* great *n* deal *pp* (of *pro* her).

2) *adj* My *n* ladies *hv* have *av* promised *pro* that *pro* I *hv* shall *adv* never *hv* be *av* sold, *conj* and *pro* I *av* have *pro* nothing —*v*— to fear; *conj* and *adv* here *adj* my *n* story *av* ends.

Paraphrase the following sentences from *Black Beauty*.
Write your answer on a seperate piece of paper.

3) There was one man, I thought, if he would buy me, I should be happy. He was not a gentleman, nor yet one of the loud, flashy sort that called themselves so. He was rather a small man, but well made, and quick in all his motions. I knew in a moment, by the way he handled me, that he was used to horses; he spoke gently, and his gray eye had a kindly, cheery look in it.

Answers on these paraphrases will vary. Evaluate them based on how many key words were actually changed and how well the paraphrase covers the original meaning.

Exercise: 13   Reinforcement Answer Key

Parse and diagram the following sentences:

———pn——— hv av pp art   n   pp art   n   pp ———pn———
4)   Black Beauty was born (in a meadow) (on the estate) (of Squire Gordon).

———adj——— adj   n   lv art   adj   n   pp art   n
5)   Black Beauty's favorite place was the beautiful meadow (at the farm).

———pn——— hv av pp   pn conj adj   n   hv   av pp ———pn———
6)   Squire Gordon could ride (on Ginger), and his wife would ride (on Black Beauty).

art adj   adj   n   hv av pp adj   n   pp adj   n
7)   The beautiful black thoroughbred was sold (to different masters) (of all sorts).

———pp——— art   n   pp adj   n   ———pn——— adv av adj   n
8)   (In spite of the difficulties) (of his life), Black Beauty always did his best.

Exercise 13: Black Beauty by Anna Sewell

4)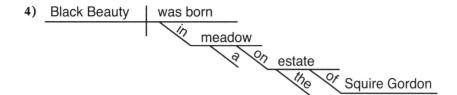

5)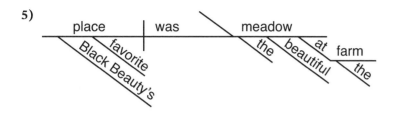

6)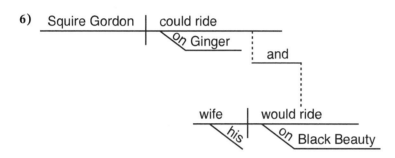

7)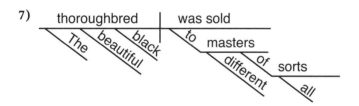

8)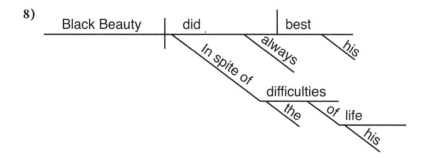

Exercise 14: "The Sword Excalibur" by Sir Thomas Malory

This story tells of some of the adventures of King Arthur and Merlin the Magician. It is written in an old-fashioned sort of English and is often hard to understand, but the stories about King Arthur are wonderful ones. There are more modern versions of these stories and legends that might be easier for you to read.

Parse the following sentences from the book:

1) ```
   pn    av  adv  ——pn——  conj  av  adv  pp   pro  pp  art   adj    n
   Merlin took up King Arthur and rode forth (with him) (upon the knight's horse).
   ```

2) ```
   adv  ——pn——  conj  pn   av      av    adj    n    pp  adj   n   conj  av
   So King Arthur and Merlin alighted, tied their horses (to two trees), and went
   
   pp   art   n
   (into the barge).
   ```

Paraphrase the following sentences from "The Sword Excalibur."
Write your answer on a seperate piece of paper.

3) They saw a damsel going upon the lake. "What damsel is that?" said the king.

   "That is the Lady of the Lake," said Merlin, "and within that lake is a reach [a small island], and therein is as fair a place as any is on earth, and richly beseen; and this damsel will come to you anon, and then speak fair to her that she will give you that sword."

   Therewith came the damsel to King Arthur and saluted him, and he her again.

Answers on these paraphrases will vary. Evaluate them based on how many key words were actually changed and how well the paraphrase covers the original meaning.

REINFORCEMENT ANSWER KEY **EXERCISE: 14**

Parse and diagram the following sentences:

    ——pn——   lv   art   adj   adj   n   pp   adj   pn

4)   King Arthur was the great legendary king (of ancient Britain).

     pro   hv   conj   hv   adv   hv   lv   adj   conj   pro   av   n   pp   pro

5)   He may or may not have been real, but we love stories (about him).

     ——adj——   adj   n   av   pro   adj   n

6)   King Arthur's famous sword won him many battles.

     pn   lv   art   adv   adj   n   conj   pro   av   pn   adj   adj   n

7)   Merlin was a very wise magician, and he gave Arthur much good advice.

     ——adj——   n   pp   art   adj   ——pn——   hv   av   pp   pn

8)   King Arthur's castle (with the famous Round Table) was located (in Camelot.)

Exercise 14: "The Sword Excalibur" by Sir Thomas Malory

4)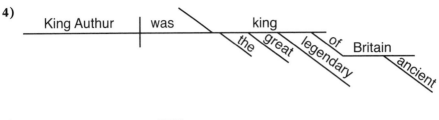

5)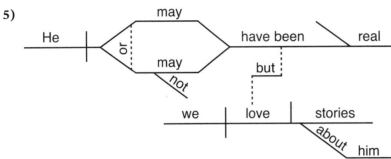

6)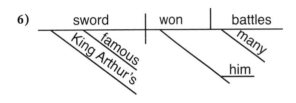

7)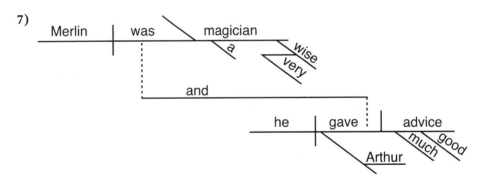

8)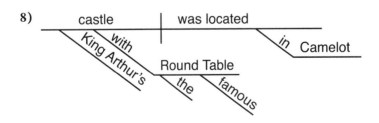

Exercise 15: *The Hobbit, or There and Back Again* by J.R.R. Tolkien

Hobbits are creatures in Tolkien's elaborate fantasy world that love home, comfort, food, and predictability. Bilbo Baggins, the hero of *The Hobbit*, turns his back on all of that and sets off on an epic adventure with a wizard and twelve dwarves.

Parse the following sentences from the book:

    pro *pro* *art*   *adj*   *pn* *av* *adj*   *n*   *lv* *art* *adj*   *n*   *pp* *art*   *n*

1) All that the unsuspecting Bilbo saw that morning was an old man (with a staff).

   pro *hv*   *av*   *pp*   *pro*   ——*v*—— *pp* *art*   *n*   *pro* *pro* *hv*   *av*   *conj pro/lv*

2) "I am looking (for someone) to share (in an adventure) that I am arranging, and it's

   adv   *adj*   ——*v*——   *pro*

very difficult to find anyone."

Remember, when parsing or diagramming contractions, identify the jobs of the words they are made of.

Paraphrase the following passage from *The Hobbit*:

Write your answer on a seperate piece of paper.

3) "Good morning!" he said at last. "We don't want any adventures here, thank you! You might try over The Hill or across The Water." By this he meant that the conversation was at an end.

"What a lot of things you do use *Good morning* for!" said Gandalf. "Now you mean that you want to get rid of me, and it won't be good till I move off."

"Not at all, not at all, my dear sir! Let me see, I don't think I know your name?"

"Yes, yes, my dear sir—and I do know your name, Mr. Bilbo Baggins. And you do know my name, though you don't remember that I belong to it. I am Gandalf, and Gandalf means me! To think that I should have lived to be good-morninged by Belladonna Took's son, as if I was selling buttons at the door!"

Answers on these paraphrases will vary. Evaluate them based on how many key words were actually changed and how well the paraphrase covers the original meaning.

EXERCISE: 15   REINFORCEMENT ANSWER KEY

Parse and diagram the following sentences:

    ———pn———   lv art adj   n   conj   adj   n   hv adv av

4) Bilbo Baggins was a respectable hobbit, and respectable hobbits did not go

   pp   n

(on adventures).

    pn   av   pn pp adj n   pp   n   conj pn   hv adv av   n

5) Gandalf wanted Bilbo (for his team) (of adventurers,) and Bilbo could not say "no."

   ———pn———   lv art adj   n   pp art   n   conj pro av   adj

6) Thorin Oakenshield was the exiled king (of the dwarves), and he sought his

   adj   n

hereditary treasure.

  pn   pn   pn   conj adj   n   av adj   adj   n   pp art

7) Bilbo, Gandalf, Thorin, and their companions had many hair-raising adventures (in the

   adj   n   pp   pn

strange world) (of Middle-earth).

   pn   av adj   n   conj art   n   hv   av   ———pn———

8) Bilbo wrote his memoirs, and the book was called *There and Back Again*.

Exercise 15:
The Hobbit, or There and Back Again by J.R.R. Tolkien

4)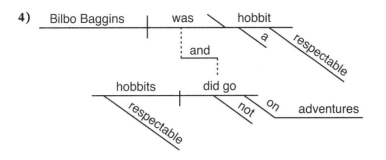

5)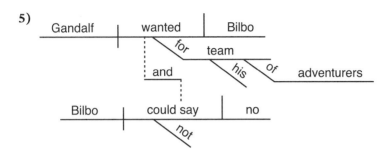

6)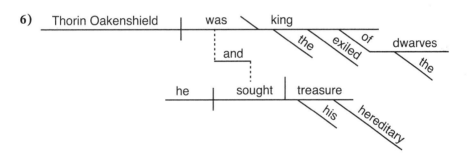

7)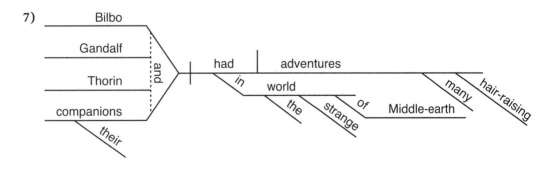

8)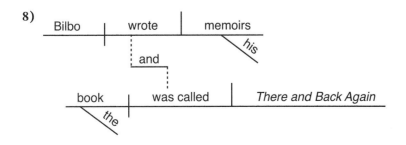

Exercise: 16 Reinforcement Answer Key

Exercise 16: *Anne of Green Gables* by Lucy Maude Montgomery

This is the story of an orphan girl who is adopted by an elderly brother and sister. Anne's sweet nature and vivid imagination change their lives considerably!

Parse the following sentences from the book:

1) When her eyes fell (on the odd little figure) (in the stiff, ugly dress), (with the
      adv adj n av pp art adj adj n pp art adj adj n pp art

   long braids (of red hair) and the eager luminous eyes), she stopped short
    adj n pp adj n conj art adj adj n pro av adv

   (in amazement.)
    pp n

   Note: *This sentence includes a prepositional phrase within a prepositional phrase; be careful!*

2) Mrs. Allan took a mouthful (of her cake) and a most peculiar expression crossed
   ——pn—— av art n pp adj n conj art adv adj n av

   her face.
    adj n

Paraphrase the following from *Anne of Green Gables*:
Write your answer on a seperate piece of paper.

3) "Anne Shirley, whatever is the matter with you? What have you done? Get right up this minute and tell me. This minute, I say. There now, what is it?"

   Anne had slid to the floor in despairing obedience.

   "Look at my hair, Marilla," she whispered.

   Accordingly, Marilla lifted her candle and looked scrutinizingly at Anne's hair, flowing in heavy masses down her back. It certainly had a very strange appearance.

   "Anne Shirley, what have you done to your hair? Why, it's green!"

   Answers on these paraphrases will vary. Evaluate them based on how many key words were actually changed and how well the paraphrase covers the original meaning.

Reinforcement Answer Key **Exercise: 16**

Parse and diagram the following sentences:

     pn   *conj* *pn*   *av*   *n* *pp* *art* *n*   *conj* *pro*   *av*   *art* *adj*   *n*

4) Matthew and Marilla needed help (on the farm), and they adopted an orphan boy.

    art   *n*   *pp* *art* *adj*   *n*   *lv* *adv* *art* *adj* *n*   *pp* *adj*   *n*

5) The "boy" (at the train station) was really a little girl (with red hair).

    adj ——*pn*——   *adv*   *av*   *art*   *n*   *pp*   *pn*   *conj*   *pn*

6) Young Anne Shirley completely changed the lives (of Matthew and Marilla).

    adj   *adj*   *n*   *conj*   *adj*   *n*   *av* *pro* *pp* *adj*   *n*

7) Anne's vivid imagination and impetuous nature led her (to many adventures).

    pn   *av*   *pp*   *art*   *pn*   *conj* *adv* *pro* *av* *art* *adj*   *n*

8) Anne stayed (with the Cuthberts), and then she had a wonderful life.

Exercise 16:
Anne of Green Gables by Lucy Maude Montgomery

4)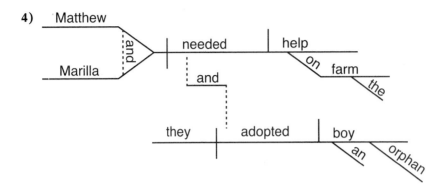

5)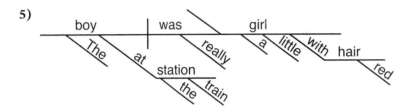

6)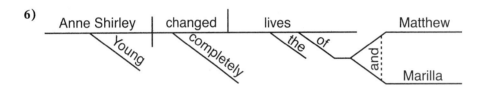

7)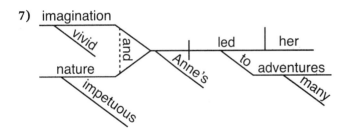

8)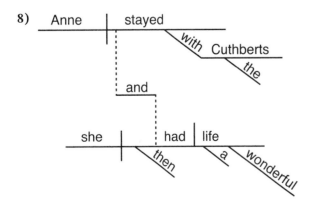

REINFORCEMENT ANSWER KEY   EXERCISE: 17

Exercise 17: *When We Were Very Young* by A. A. Milne

This exercise is from a book of children's poems. Mr. Milne wrote many stories about Christopher Robin and his favorite bear (of the Teddy variety) named Winnie the Pooh.

Parse the following sentences from the book:

1)   *pro/hv*   *av*   *n* *pp* ————*pn*———— *conj* ————*pn*———— *av*
They're changing guard (at Buckingham Palace), and Christopher Robin went

   adv *pp* *pn*
down (with Alice).

2) *pn* *lv* *art*   *n*   *art* *adj* *adj* *n*   *pn* *lv* *art* *n* *pp* *art* *adj*
Ernest was an elephant, a great big fellow; Leonard was a lion (with a six-foot

  n   *pn*   *lv* *art* *n* *conj* *adj* *n*   *lv* *adj* *conj* *pn* *lv* *art* *adv* *adj* *n*
tail); George was a goat, and his head was yellow; and James was a very small snail.

Paraphrase the following from *When We Were Very Young*:
Write your answer on a seperate piece of paper.

3) Whenever I walk in a London Street,
   I'm ever so careful to watch my feet;
        And I keep in the squares,
        And the masses of bears,
   Who wait at the corners all ready to eat
   The sillies who tread on the lines of the street, Go
        back to their lairs,
        And I say to them, "Bears,
        Just look how I'm walking in all of the squares!"

Answers on these paraphrases will vary. Evaluate them based on how many key words were actually changed and how well the paraphrase covers the original meaning.

EXERCISE: 17   REINFORCEMENT ANSWER KEY

Parse and diagram the following sentences:

    pp   n   ———pn———   av   adj   n   conj   n   pp   n

4) (For decades), A. A. Milne wrote many poems and stories (for children).

    ———pn———   lv art n   pp art   n   conj pro lv art   n

5) "Daffodowndilly" is a poem (about a daffodil) and it is a favorite.

    art   adj   n   pp adj   n   av art adj   n   pp art   n   pp pn

6) The central character (in these poems) has a great friend (by the name) (of Pooh).

    ———pn———   av   adj   n conj adj adv   adj   pro lv   ———pn———

7) Christopher Robin has many toys, and his very favorite one is Winnie the Pooh.

    ———pn——— hv   lv   adj   pp   n   conj adj   n   pp art adv adj   n

8) A. A. Milne has been popular (with children and their parents) (for a very long time).

Exercise 17: *When We Were Very Young* by A. A. Milne

4)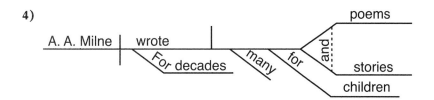

5)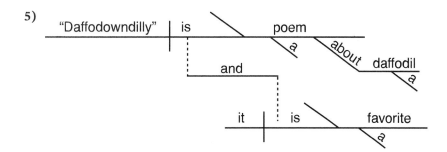

6)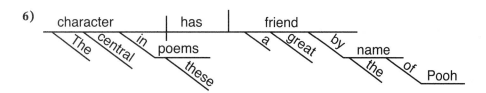

7)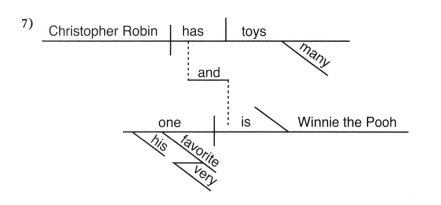

8)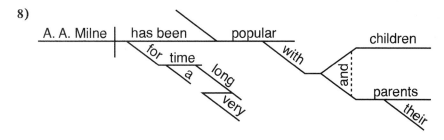

Exercise 18: *Mary Poppins* by P. L. Travers

This collection of short stories tells of the adventures of Jane and Michael Banks, two little English children, and their extraordinary and magical nanny.

Parse the following sentences from the book:

    adv   pp art   n   pn conj pn   av   pp art   n   conj

1) Upstairs (in the nursery), Jane and Michael watched (at the window) and

    av   pro   hv   av

   wondered who would come.

    pp   adj adj   n   pp adj   n   pro av   adv   pp art   n   conj

2) (With her large bag) (in her hands) she slid gracefully (UP the banisters) and

    av   pp art   n   pp art adj   n   pp ——pn——

   arrived (at the landing) (at the same time) (as Mrs. Banks).

Paraphrase the following from *Mary Poppins*:

Write your answer on a seperate piece of paper.

3) "Well," said Mary Poppins, "it's all very silly and undignified, but, since you're all up there and don't seem able to get down, I suppose I'd better come up, too."

With that, to the surprise of Jane and Michael, she put her hands down at her sides and without a laugh, without even the faintest glimmer of a smile, she shot up through the air and sat down beside Jane.

"How many times, I should like to know," she said snappily, "have I told you to take off your coat when you come into a hot room?" And she unbuttoned Jane's coat and laid it neatly on the air beside the hat.

Answers on these paraphrases will vary. Evaluate them based on how many key words were actually changed and how well the paraphrase covers the original meaning.

REINFORCEMENT ANSWER KEY — EXERCISE: 18

Parse and diagram the following sentences:

4) Jane(pn) and(conj) Michael(pn) were(lv) two(adj) children(n) (of(pp) a(art) family)(n) (on(pp) Cherry Tree Lane)(pn) (in(pp) London)(pn).

5) The(art) Bankses(pn) needed(av) a(art) new(adj) nanny(n) (for(pp) their(adj) children,)(n) and(conj) they(pro) advertised(av) (for(pp) one)(pro).

6) They(pro) put(av) an(art) advertisement(n) (in(pp) the(art) paper)(n) and(conj) hoped(av) (for(pp) a(art) well-qualified(adj) person)(n).

7) Nobody(pro) (but(pp) Mary Poppins)(pn) came(av) (to(pp) their(adj) house)(n) (in(pp) answer)(n) (to(pp) the(art) advertisement)(n).

8) She(pro) had(av) wonderful(adj) magical(adj) powers(n), and(conj) incredible(adj) things(n) always(adv) happened(av) (on(pp) an(art) outing)(n) (with(pp) her)(pro).

EXERCISE: 18   REINFORCEMENT ANSWER KEY

Exercise 18: *Mary Poppins* by P. L. Travers

4)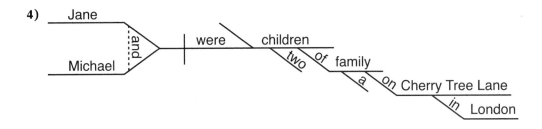

5)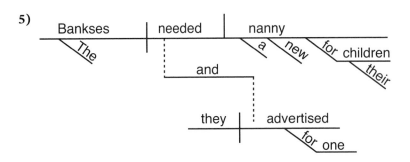

6)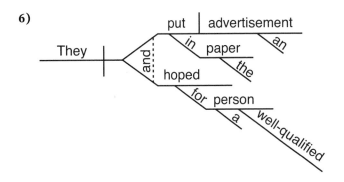

7)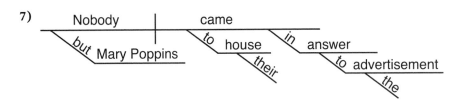

8)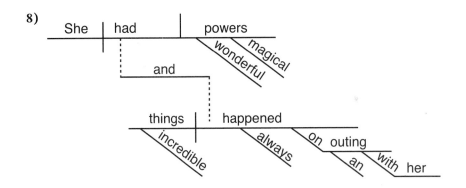

Index

Concepts are listed by lesson number.

*Indicates item is found in Application & Enrichment activity

A
abstract nouns 1
action verbs 4
adjectives 1
adverbs 5
antecedents 2
articles 1

B
broken dogleg 7

C
comma splices 4*
comma splits 8*
common nouns 1
commands 4
compound sentences 10
compound situations 10
compounds 10
conditional action 9
conjunctions 10
context 2, 3*
coordinating conjunction . . . 10
correlative conjunction 10

D
definite articles 1
demonstrative pronouns 2
direct object 6
dogleg 5

F
FANBOYS 10

H
helping verbs 9

I
indefinite articles 1
indefinite pronouns 2
indirect object 7
intensive pronouns 2
interrogative pronouns 2

L
linking verb 8

M
modals 9
modifiers 1, 3

N
N-LV-ADJ sentence 8
N-LV-N sentence 8
N-V sentence 6
N-V-N sentence 6
N-V-N-N sentence 7
nouns 1

O
object of the preposition 3
objective pronouns 2

P
paraphrasing 1*, 2*
personal pronouns 2
phrases 3
plagiarism 2*
plural pronouns 2
possessive pronouns 2
predicate 4

predicate adjective 8
predicate nominative 8
prepositional phrases 3
prepositions 3
progressive action 9
pronouns 2
proper adjectives 1
proper nouns 1

R
reflexive pronouns 2
relative pronouns 2
run-on sentence 4*

S
Sentence Pattern 1 6
Sentence Pattern 2 6
Sentence Pattern 3 7
Sentence Pattern 4 8
Sentence Pattern 5 8
sentences 4, 6
simple predicate 4
simple subject 4
singular pronouns 2
singular they 2
starting sentences with
conjunctions 10*
subject 4
subjective pronouns 2
synonyms 1*, 5*, 6*, 7*, 9*

T
tail 7
The Process (complete) 8

Index

U

understood *you* 4

V

verb 4, 8, 9

verb phrase 9

verbals 4

Bibliography

Florey, Kitty Burns. Sister Bernadette's Barking Dog: The Quirky History and Lost Art of Diagramming Sentences. Orlando, FL: Harcourt, 2007.

Garner, Bryan A. Garner's Modern English Usage. Oxford: Oxford University Press, 2016.

Garner, Bryan A. The Chicago Guide to Grammar, Usage, and Punctuation. Chicago, IL: The University of Chicago Press, 2016.

Truss, Lynne. Eats, Shoots & Leaves: The Zero Tolerance Approach to Punctuation. London: Fourth Estate, 2009.